www.ataboveandbeyond.com

Copyright © 2023 At Above And Beyond. All rights reserved. No part of this publication may be reproduced, distributed or transmuted in any form or by any means, including photocopying, recording or other electronic and mechanical methods, without the prior written permission of the publisher.

Compiled and Published by At Above And Beyond E: ataboveandbeyond@gmail.com
W: ataboveandbeyond.com

This book is for entertainment purposes only. Nothing in this book or any affiliations with this book is a substitute for legal, medical or psychological help and advice. If you are in need of help, please seek out a professional for support.

ISBN: 9798385961023

INTRODUCTION

"Forever Changed: Healing through Grief" is an apt title. Grief comes in many forms and from many different types of events in someone's life. Most often, when someone refers to grief, they are talking about the feelings and process one goes through after a death.

Within the pages of this book, you will read stories by 19 authors, whom each wanted to share a part of their own personal journey through grief. We know that in the sharing of these stories, not only will it help the authors bring healing to themselves and the experiences in their lives, but that it may also assist others during their own journeys of healing through grief.

Please remember that this book is not intended to replace professional assistance in your healing. Please reach out to a medical or trained professional to assist you if you need help.

Thank you for reading.

MAGGIE MORRIS

Maggie is an Authentic Caring, Sensitive Soul with a Passion for nurturing others with her Soul Love. Maggie lives her gifts of service to humanity through her generosity and her ability to ignite the flame in others to see their limitless possibilities. Maggie uses her intuition and connection with Spirit to be an example of strength and courage to all she meets. Now as an Author, Public Speaker, Life Coach, Mindfulness Master/Mentor, Meditation Facilitator, Government of Ontario Certified Officiant and Death Doula, Maggie continues to pursue her passions as well as help those she connects with to find Healing.
You can reach Maggie through her website at www.whispersofwisdom.ca or through Facebook.

THE GRIEF THAT FOREVER CHANGED MAGGIE BY MAGGIE MORRIS

Let me ask you......

Are you awakened to the thought that grief is part of life?

Sadness is part of Bliss?

Heartache is part of Joy?

Grief is the price we pay for Love and that ever so-deep grief is the cost of beautiful Love. We cannot escape it. We cannot run from it. We must journey with it.

If we say "I will not Grieve", we cannot Love. Grief is a part of life. Part of a life we all must live. Life is full of happy/sad experiences and both have beautiful things to teach us, yet we choose only the good. Of course, we do!

I personally think the joyous moments cushion us for the hard stuff and grief certainly is part of the hard stuff.

It would be easy to write about the clinical side of grief, the types of grief, and the stages of grief as all of those things do help us understand grief. They help us process grief on paper but the living through grief is the difficult part I want to write about.

Maggie Morris

In my lifetime I have experienced many different combinations of grief, yet I have felt blessed not to have experienced too much grief.

In my childhood years, there was the grief of not having the friend you want or possibly having friends exclude you, maybe not being chosen for the sports team. Maybe throw in the loss of a loved pet. These are all grief experiences. Not all grief is a death. As we grow up we find that Grief has many faces.

Although there are many faces of grief, I believe the greatest grief that profoundly changes us is the loss through the death of a deeply treasured loved one. It could be a parent, a grandparent, a partner, a soulmate, a close friend, a sibling, a child or even on occasion a pet that is more than just a pet. Yes, we can be forever changed by the loss of a pet.

Whatever the grief, it is that deep loss that you feel in your gut like a bomb has just exploded and you have a gaping hole in your life you cannot fill. Just reading these words makes you feel it all over again.

Yes, that's the type of grief that forever changes you.
For me, that grief was the loss of my mother.

My mother; the woman that knew me before I was me. That woman; who loved me before I was me. That woman; who truly knew me but loved me anyway.

Maggie Morris

My mother; she was my best friend. In my younger years, she was my protector. She was that soft shoulder to lean on for comfort, she got me! She was that safe place that I could retreat to when my world got too hard. She softened the bumps of life. I was not prepared for her to be gone. I was not prepared for her to get sick and helpless. I was not prepared for life without a mother. I was so blessed that the time did not come for me until I was in my fifties. Yet even though her death came in my fifties, I still became that little girl who wanted her mommy. That grief was deep! It profoundly rocked my life!

We are never prepared for grief. Oh, I know, sometimes we think we are. When that loved one has been sick for a long time we can experience anticipatory grief.

Anticipatory grief is similar to the normal process of mourning, but it happens before the actual death. It is in anticipation of the death.

I experienced that anticipatory grief with my mom as she was actively in the dying process for about four months, with the last six weeks of her life in a medically induced coma. That anticipatory process is like holding your breath as the glass full of milk falls off the table, you know the bang is coming, and you're even prepared for it, yet when the glass hits the floor and breaks spattering milk all over, you still jump like you had no idea it was coming.

It was a few months after her death that I decided I needed to do some work on myself. I remember it like yesterday! I was standing on my front porch on New Year's Eve 2017 and declared to the Universe that 2018 was going to be my year of healing. Little did I know that one single moment in time would change my life forever! The next day, being New Year's Day, I had an opportunity to speak to both of my adult children and I remember telling them that I was going on this Journey of Healing. I told them I would be taking care of me for the next year and might be a little distracted from life. Wow! Was that ever true! That year fundamentally changed me to my core. Did you know that when you ask the universe for help, the universe shows up!

That year brought so many opportunities for healing and unpacking layers of myself that I never even knew existed. I had been living on autopilot for so long that I completely lost my true identity, yet I knew I was going to make it my mission to find myself. I was going on a mission to find the true Maggie. I was going to go deep to find her true essence! That was the moment in time when my Grief would Forever Change Me!

I remember, at some point in the process, meeting a therapist, going to see her only to find myself paying her to have her tell me that I needed to look inside myself, that everything I needed was already within. She told me that I simply needed to find the keys to unlock the doors with all the answers. One day, she asked a simple question that rocked me to my core. She asked what made me happy? I had no idea! How sad that in my fifty years, if I had known what made me happy, I had somehow forgotten because I had absolutely no idea how to find the answer to her question to me that day. That question sent me on a quest to find out what truly did make me happy. What was happiness for that matter?

A few years later, through a lot of soul searching, combined with working on my inner self, I discovered that happiness is not found in a place or an emotion. Happiness is found within! I discovered that when I learned to Love & Accept myself, I found true happiness. Please, don't misunderstand the point I write about, as yes, we do feel happiness in moments treasured by experiences of joy with others, or events in life, but true lasting happiness does come only through Love & Acceptance of one's self.

That Journey of Grief at the loss of my mom propelled me into a greater life change that has and is Forever Changing Maggie!

When we grieve we have a choice to make in that grief. How will grief change us? Will it make us better or bitter? Grief is a long journey of healing but I have found that it can also be a pivotal life-changing moment that propels us to search deeper into the meaning of life.

If you find yourself experiencing deep grief at this time in your life please know, that you are not alone. Please know, that Grief is Love with nowhere to go. Please know, that you will get through it. You get through it by allowing yourself to grieve. You get through it by not rushing the process. You get through it by being gentle with yourself. You get through it, by giving grief your time. Grief is not something you get over, it's something you journey through. Grief is something that will "Forever Change You" as you learn to live and create a new life without that someone you Love.

Now almost six years after the death of my beloved momma, I facilitate grief groups and help others in their journey through grief. This grief journey of mine has propelled me to wake up every day and live life fully. I now follow the passions of my soul and allow Spirit to be my guide as I walk through the rest of my years on this earth.

To quote Bréne Brown….."**I plan to live out the rest of my life standing in the light of vulnerability** and authenticity — and I will embrace anyone who courageously meets me there."

Will you meet me there?

Sending you much Love for that journey, and if you need a supportive listening ear please reach out.

Maggie Morris

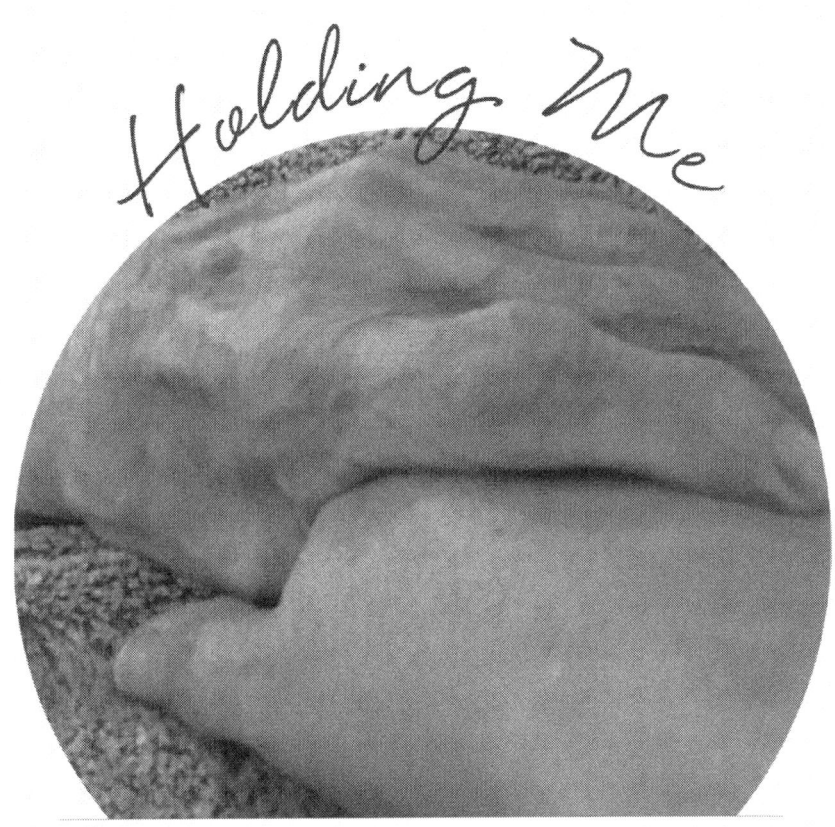

BUNNY KEATING

Bunny is a mother, widow, daughter, sister, friend, entrepreneur, healer, coach, author, mentor and public speaker. She has chosen to see the gifts in all of life's experiences, even the ones which are painful, and she has decided to live a life full of joy, happiness, laughter and love.

You can reach her by email bunnykeating@gmail.com

MY FOREVER CHANGED
BY BUNNY KEATING

I opened my eyes and looked up towards him, the same thing I'd been doing for weeks, checking on him while he was lying in a hospital bed in what used to be our dining room, but was now a different place. It was no longer a caring and loving space where dreams of glorious futures were being had. It had become 'clinical.'

My blood ran cold, as my internal voice screamed in extreme agony, "OH NO!" My nightmare had become a reality, his chest wasn't rising. He wasn't breathing anymore.

I jumped up faster than I could even fathom being able to move and I got into action. I called 9-1-1. I turned on the dining room light. I went to the front door to unlock it, having remembered this from my CPR training class, which I took 4 days after my dad died from a heart attack 5 years earlier.

I was answering the operator's questions. I was in "action" mode.

You see, I'm great in a crisis. My mind becomes laser focused. It's about survival. There's always time for me to freak out and break down later. Now is the time for doing!

I was speaking to the operator, following her instructions. I got Steve down onto the floor and started chest compressions. I could hear the bones cracking........

Bunny Keating

I remembered this from that same training class too....."If you do CPR correctly, you will break their ribs. Broken ribs are better than death." I kept going.

I also remembered another thing from the training class, "CPR is less successful in restarting an adult's heart on its own. You are moving the blood around the body, until someone can come with the defibrillator, to give them a chance of surviving without brain damage from a lack of oxygen, if their heart can be restarted."

I remember being amazed at how quickly I became sore and tired from performing the compressions. I remember it feeling like it took FOREVER for the firefighters to show up. Me hearing the knock on the door and calling out, "Come in." The greatest sense of relief that help had finally arrived. I was spent. I did my absolute best. My best wasn't enough.

I don't know how the transition happened from me pushing on his chest, acting as the heartbeat of my love, to me sitting in the stairway while other people were doing their job, trying to save a life. That part is sort of a hazy fog. I guess our minds do that to protect us. Lessen the trauma.

I held out hope that Steve would survive right up until the moment I watched the backs of the EMS team silently leaving, not making eye contact with me. It was unnecessary for the Police Officer to tell me that Steve was dead, but he still did it, it must be a part of his job. The official declaration, "I'm sorry, but he didn't make it."

Bunny Keating

I don't remember much about what was said, luckily my mind protected me from a lot of the details of this trauma.

I remember thinking that it was weird that they didn't take his body. Apparently, we were waiting for the coroner, or our family doctor to come and officially pronounce him dead. Neither were answering their phones. They never did come. Then the police officer asked which funeral home we were to call. My sister had to answer that question for me, I couldn't even remember the name of one. It was too much to handle.

I stayed in the stairway until the funeral home came. All I could think about was saving myself from the added trauma of watching them carry his body out of our home. I knew that I was already going to have enough memories from tonight that would never leave me, like the fact that Steve's unblinking eyes were open when I checked on him. Thankfully, he had turned his head away. One final gift of love from the man I loved with all of my heart.

I went out to my sister's car with my mom and my friend, Stephanie(she being the person I called after the firefighters arrived). I asked my sister to drive down the street a little bit. I didn't want to leave him, but I also couldn't watch. I couldn't bare witness as the love of my life was being taken away. After the nondescript van pulled out of the driveway and the last police cruiser left, we went back inside. The first thing I noticed was how quiet it was. No more oxygen machine, or air compressor for the hospital bed air mattress making their mechanical sounds. Just deafening silence. My ears actually ached from it. A silence I have never experienced before or since.

In that moment, I knew something had changed. My life would never look the same. After 10 months of chemo, radiation, doctor's appointments, emergency room trips, painkillers, home nurse visits, etc the life we were trying to hold onto was done. Now I was going onto a new future. One where I was alone.

My future was now forever changed.

****

You know what is one of the hardest things to do after a loss? Telling others.

I couldn't say the words to anyone but Stephanie, so she stepped up and helped me by making the calls to the people who needed to know.

She called Steve's mom to tell her. She called my mom, my sister, the nurses, his work, and my work......but we couldn't tell everyone right away. You see, my oldest son, Christopher was at a boxing tournament in Toronto, and he was going to be fighting that night. I didn't want him to be preoccupied with Steve's death while in the ring. I didn't tell my other friends. I didn't post about it on any socials out of fear that Topher would find out from someone else.

Bunny Keating

It was hard to deal with my grief privately without the support of those I needed most. My public grieving had to wait.

It felt like the silence had compounded exponentially.

The next day, I decided to go to the tournament and hide from my son so I could watch him from the other side of the event space. I knew he would know something happened to Steve if he saw me. I waited outside in the cold, in the parking lot, until I knew his fight was next. I walked through the door, crossed the hallway, stepped into the event space, and turned left, only to be faced with my son walking directly towards me, only about 10 feet away. He smiled. I smiled and told him to have a good fight. Topher later said that for a moment, when he saw me, he thought, "How is she here," but he quickly re-focused on his task ahead.

When he stepped into the ring, I saw that he was wearing the boxing shoes Steve had given him. It was the first time he had worn them. Tears silently streamed down my face. My sons lost someone special too. They lost someone they loved.

Telling my sons that Steve died was so incredibly hard.

Their lives were also forever changed.

****

Bunny Keating

A funny thing happens after someone dies. Okay, not funny "ha-ha," more like funny in the way that it is weird.

Immediately after Steve died, I had a crippling fear that someone else I loved would die. I was extremely afraid that one of my children would die. And they would die immediately. I have had fears of them dying in the past and I usually can talk my mind into erasing the fear, or at least pushing it aside for a bit, but now this was not possible. It was like my survival instinct did not want to get hurt any more than I already was, and I was looking to control the dangers around those I loved, to protect myself.

I wanted my children around me every moment. If they weren't around me, I needed to be able to contact them and make sure they were okay. Luckily, they understood.

I had heard about the steps you go through in grief. I had even grieved before. I didn't remember ever hearing about the crippling fear you can experience where now you think everyone is going to die too.

This is something I spoke to others about. I learned that I was in fact quite normal. Over time, this feeling lessened. It has never truly disappeared, but it's manageable.

In this way, like countless others, I am forever changed.

****

Nine days after Steve died, I had to return to work. I was a single mom again, with only one income. There were young mouths to feed and a roof to keep over their heads. I couldn't freeze life. It keeps going, even as our loved ones are missing.

Going back to work created obstacles of its own. How was I going to get through my breaks at work since I always called to talk to him? How would I decompress after work without being able to share my stories with him? Who was going to drive me in when it snowed?

Who was going to tell the co-workers whom I'd see and would ask me about Steve and how he was doing? I dreaded having to tell people the "news" over and over again. Each time it was like a hot poker stabbing through my gaping wound.

My work life was forever changed.

****

In the five-plus years since Steve died, I have gone on to have some incredible experiences. I have watched both of my sons graduate from High School. I have watched my eldest son graduate from a four-year college program. I have met the daughter of my heart(my eldest son's girlfriend). I travelled to Scotland with my sister for a week of magic. I sold my house, the one we shared together and created memories in. I expanded and embraced my spiritual gifts(Steve still communicates with me through my mediumship). I got the job of my dreams, only to find out it wasn't what I wanted. I started 3 businesses. I have learned. I have healed. I have grown. I have laughed. I have cried.

Most of all, I have been forever changed.

****

The biggest takeaway I have from the death of Steve is that I wish I had spent more time relishing every delicious moment. I always thought we would have more time, later. We could do that, later. I could record him singing karaoke, later. I'd remember his story better, later. Our laters are no more.

My outlook on life is forever changed.

****

So today, as a way to honour Steve, before you go to sleep, I ask you to reach out to someone you love and tell them. Let them know how amazing they are. How much they mean to you. How grateful you are that they are in your life. How they make your world a better place. Let that be the legacy of our love story, the one I have shared with you today. Love matters. Love never dies. Love is eternal.

Love also leaves you Forever Changed.

Bunny Keating

"LIFE IS SHORT, SO GIVE IT ALL YOU'VE GOT" ~ THE JAY DIEM BAND

SARAH WHITE

Sarah White was born and raised in Niagara Falls, Ontario. She is a proud Educational Assistant for individuals having intellectual disabilities in a local french high school.
During 2022, she experienced many "firsts." She purchased her first car and moved into her first apartment. Sarah is thrilled to add being a first-time collaborative author to her list and is proud to join the group of authors in her family. She dedicates this chapter to anybody who has or has had a loved one with dementia.

"Live every day one step at a time and remember to soak in every moment you have with them. To my "sunshine," my grandmother, Eleanor White, you are so loved and missed. This is for you!

MY ONLY SUNSHINE
BY SARAH WHITE

I think we take many things for granted in life. For example, the ability to know how to make coffee in the morning; the ability to make our own decisions; the ability to invite and receive your family and friends for dinner; or the ability to remember family memories without much concern. Individuals who live with dementia can't experience these things as freely. For those of you who aren't very familiar, "Dementia" is an umbrella term for similar diseases that affect the brain such as Parkinson's and early-onset Alzheimer's. Over the course of time, the brain will start to cognitively decline and the individual will start to lose the ability to perform everyday tasks independently and simply "forget."

If you have a loved one who is diagnosed with dementia, you understand that it not only affects the individual diagnosed but the families and caregivers as well. Caring for them, slowly watching someone you love start to cognitively decline and living in fear of not remembering where they are, who they are, or who we are is not easy at all. I know for me, it tugged at my heartstrings. It was very hard to watch my grandmother go through this. Let's backtrack a few years, as I share about my relationship with her and her journey with dementia.

Grandma was trying to balance out her new lifestyle after some major changes happened in her life. The two major ones were my grandfather passing away and then her

Sarah White

moving from the home they had lived in for over 50 years, and into a small condo completely on her own. Unfortunately, being there caused her to become depressed. My dad and his brothers quickly came to the realization that she needed to be living somewhere where she had around-the-clock care, and other people to live with. Thankfully, transferring her to this new home was the right decision. She was happier there, and she was very receptive to the other residents. I will always remember the friend she made, her name was Goldie. Goldie was always looking out for my grandmother. They watched television and ate together. They really were the best of friends. I was happy to know that my grandma wasn't alone.

Grandma also kept a journal and wrote in it every day. I remember her always writing about who came to visit her each day. She had such beautiful handwriting. I can still see it when I look at an old recipe book, in which she made personal notes beside her favourite recipes. My dad always told me she made the best pies.

Until one day, she fell and suffered a stroke...
Over the course of time, my parents started to notice she was becoming slightly forgetful about small details. Fast forward a couple of years and she was really struggling with recognizing where she was, who was around her and being able to answer basic questions such as, "What did you have for breakfast today?" It was sad to see, but our weekly Sunday visits with her at the home became a routine I never wanted to miss. We chatted about what we did during the week. My sister and I always updated her on what we were up to and how we were doing in school. Although it seemed

Sarah White

like she was following the conversation, I felt that she had no clue what was being said. In between conversations, she would interrupt and ask who it was she was with.

Sometimes, if we were telling her that we would go for a short walk, she would start to panic and ask where we were taking her, and if she'd be back in time for dinner.

The more I think about it today, it hurts me to know how confused she was and even though she was constantly reassured by her caregivers and family, she never "knew" for sure. Despite the memory loss, my grandmother was the sweetest lady and she had a spunky personality. She knew how to make you laugh in a situation that was genetically sad. She used to repeat the same questions over and over and I remember just answering them over and over. Also, when she would bring up stories of her past, we would just "play along" and live in her "reality" at that moment. I began to realize that it didn't really matter how true the story. Spending quality time with her was what mattered to me. Now, on to my favourite moments with her. I know my grandma was loved by many, but my connection with her was different. She had me wrapped around her little finger. My grandmother used to sing in a church choir and I also love to sing. One thing I started to do with her when she was starting to become frustrated was to break up the conversation by singing nursery rhymes, "The Itsy bitsy spider", and "My little teacup." But our favourite one to sing was "You are my Sunshine." It became "our thing." This was our special connection, so much so that I have "You are my Sunshine" tattooed on my forearm.

Sarah White

On August 31st, 2016, grandma passed away peacefully in her chair. That's the day my healing began.

I wish I could thank her today for the impact that she had on me and my life. Thanks to her, I realized what I wanted to do for my post-secondary studies and it eventually led to the career that I have now. She taught me that music is a way of healing through good times and bad. When she had her bad days, singing made us both feel better. During her funeral, we played a recording of the two of us singing our song, and in a way, I was sad hearing that while we were laying her to rest, but it also made me feel so much love because I knew she was in a better place. I'll have that moment to hold forever.

Sarah White

I continue to grieve her loss and I am thankful for every moment shared with her. She taught me many life lessons over time. The lesson that will always resonate with me is the importance of playing music and how it can bring people together. Thanks to my grandma, the meaning of the song "You are my sunshine" has a whole different meaning. I am forever changed.

BETTY LONG

Betty is a sensitive caring nurturing soul with the heart of a mother. The oldest of five children, she learned at a young age to be a nurturing leader to her siblings. As a Special Needs Educational Assistant, she continued with that nurturing energy. Married to the same man for 51 and a half years, she has learned a thing or two about commitment along the way. All her adult life, there has always been room at Betty's table for someone needing Love and occasionally, even a few moved in. Now retired and widowed, Betty is embarking on a new journey of discovering what is next for her. Certainly, through her commitment to her Faith, that sensitive, caring and nurturing soul will emerge once again.

GRIEF CHANGES EVERYTHING
BY BETTY LONG

Grief is the price you pay for loving and being loved deeply! It never ends, you just learn how to live without the person. All the love you had for the person is still there but there is no way to express it, or you don't know how to do that yet. Everything I am has changed!

I have lost grandparents, parents and others but none of the losses compared to the loss of my husband. It was the loss of my best friend, my comfort, the love of my life...my constant companion for over fifty-one years. It has created a void, the deepest void which I can't ever see being filled. When my mother was dying, after a lengthy illness, I remember how concerned she was for her children who would be left behind. So when my husband Dave was dying I assured him, "It's okay to die because the same God who guided and protected us for 51 years of marriage will continue to keep me and the family after your death." Little did I realize how difficult that would be! How long it would last? Sometimes I feel like I am just existing, other times I feel that I can do this, but one thing is for sure, I know I could not do this without God!

At first, it seemed like I was running on autopilot. Sometimes a smell or a song would trigger the grief and I would start to cry. Even seeing a couple shopping together in the grocery store, often I would stop shopping and just leave the store overcome by my grief.

Now, a year later there is still an empty space in my life. Sometimes the loneliness just creeps up on me.

The good memories come to mind often and then blast in the realization that he is gone, never coming back with an empty spot in my heart that never goes away, and it feels like it will never be okay. Some days almost feel normal, but then like the waves of the ocean, grief hits like a bad storm, leaving you feeling totally broken.

Shortly after David's death, I joined a Grief Share group. This helped a lot because I realized that I was not going crazy. All of the things I was experiencing were normal for many people grieving. It also helped to hear success stories from those who had survived their grief experience.

I learned that everyone's experience with grief has similarities, however many times there are differences. Like guilt, anger, and regret, these don't run in any order, you can never say, "I'm done with that part of my grief." There's no timeline for the beginning, after the numbness stage has ended, and so far, I can't say there is an end to the grief. Grief sometimes makes you feel like you're in a dense fog, you feel empty, lonely and useless. There are also times when you have a pity party. "Why me?" "Will this ever end?" "No one else will ever love me like he did?" Even the, "I have nothing to live for" stage. When these thoughts come, it is best to change your thinking and remind yourself of things you have to be thankful for. It might even help to make a Thankful List on a good day and reread the list on a negative day. Reading the Bible or praying is also a good release.

Betty Long

I have found you just have to learn to live a new life without your loved one. Discover a different YOU! Your life is totally different. Sometimes people who you thought were friends just seem to drop out of your life. Others are totally there for you! I have some friends who send me words of encouragement almost weekly, this is often a real pick me up.

You have to remember that those around you are also dealing with their own grief. You can not carry their grief, that is something they need to do, all you can do is try to understand them and give them space to grieve in their own way. This is difficult when it is your children, no matter how old they are.

I have recently formed a Grief Share Group at our church and am presently facilitating the group of 10 people. We are each working through our grief together. Helping them is helping me to continue to work with my grief.

Christmas was difficult! There were so many memories of Christmases past and longing for what is missing now. The realization that he will never be here again, the sadness and loss of that special relationship. Each holiday brings new memories, new sorrows, and new emptiness. Life goes on but people don't realize the loss and loneliness that you experience. The loss of companionship becomes so real, especially during the holidays. Every time you come across something that your person owned or enjoyed there is a fresh reminder of your loss. Every day is a new experience, one day at a time sometimes one minute at a time! Some days you think, "I can do this," and other days you feel like you can't take another step or breathe another breath. Then in a moment, I'm reminded of an old song... "You're gonna make it, you've got what it takes ...as long as you and Jesus stay friends." Sometimes you feel like no one cares and even God isn't there but trust me, He is there all of the time. Your feelings are just blocking you from knowing and seeing. He is there.

Does the death of a loved one Forever Change You? It sure does! In my experience, it shakes you to the core and makes you question everything in your life. It causes you to wonder what's real and what isn't. It makes you feel tested on every level. It makes you wonder if you will survive this experience. It changes your outlook on everything in your life and leaves you feeling inside out and upside down. You soon realize you are stronger than you thought, even though it's the biggest test of your life. You will make it. You will learn to stand on your own two feet. You will succeed, and you will be stronger for having passed through this Valley of the shadow of death.

Has grief changed me? What does the next picture of me look like? I am still in the middle of this process but it will surely change me! How? I'm not sure. Most of the time the pain is less than before. Sometimes it seems worse. Like a caterpillar in a cocoon, I am changing. I will be different. Sometimes I feel like I am only half here. If when you marry, two become one, then when one dies, are you left as one half? Eventually the new whole you will arrive. A stronger you for the grief battle you have fought. So keep moving through the process and become the New Stronger You!

Betty Long

ROSE BOURASSA

Rose Bourassa had a distinguished career as a procurement specialist. Away from work, she has worn many hats: mother, grandmother, student, and teacher. Recently retired, she has become an international bestselling author and serves her community by volunteering with her local library and, most recently, the local Relay for Life Team. She holds board offices with both groups. She strives to learn something new every day to keep her mind sharp and interact with her grandkids to keep her young at heart. She is currently preparing for a second career as an evidential medium.
You can contact Rose via email at remnick@aol.com

FOREVER CHANGED
BY ROSE BOURASSA

Years ago, I lost my son in a tragic accident. He died on a Thursday, the week before Thanksgiving. Those first days were a blur as I tried to navigate all of the details in preparing for his final send-off. There were many people to talk to: the police, the coroner, the funeral home, family, and friends. We had a never-ending stream of people coming and going through our house.

Getting through those first holidays was a challenge. We began life with our new normal when all the dust had settled. Without him, things would never be the same again. We knew that, and we dealt with it daily.

A friend suggested that we, as a family, attend grief counselling to help us get through the craziness and maybe make some sense of it all. My husband did not feel the need for that, so my daughter and I went without him. Our first group session was tough. We listened to everyone's story of their loss before sharing our own. As newcomers to the group, we received a lot of sympathy and condolences. I do not recall that first session making me feel better about my loss, but I did return for another session.

The second session appeared to repeat the first, but I was a bit more aware of what was being said and who was saying it. My daughter and I had not yet made it to the 90-day mark, and here we were, in a support group with people who had been coming for years. That just boggled my mind. I could not comprehend why you needed years of support.

We stayed with the group for three months. Our attention was on the woman who had lost her husband. From how she talked, I thought she'd lost him about the same time I lost my son. This woman could not get herself out of bed in the morning. She lost her job and was about to lose her home. She no longer had any income. She did not know how to pay her bills or tend to things around the house. Her husband had done everything for her. Her share time involved usage of several boxes of tissue. When she said that he husband died two years ago, my jaw hit the floor!

As we drove home that night, my daughter and I talked about her. Neither of us could understand the depths of her grief and how she had not been able to move forward in two years. I shared this story with the friend who suggested this support group: She was as perplexed as I was. At about that same time, I decided to write my son a letter and let him know how angry and hurt I was that he had left us. Writing everything helped me understand my feelings and how I needed to deal with them. Writing would be the turning point in my grief process. That single letter turned into half a notebook of notes and letters. Whenever I remembered a cute story about him, I wrote it down. I wrote down all the things he did in life that angered me. It made me deal with the happy, the sad and the angry all at the same time.

The notebook did more for me to heal my heart and soul than the support group did. In the last group we attended, I

Rose Bourassa

shared that I had started journaling and was considering turning my journal into a book about my son. The entire group ordered a copy.

In the group, I learned that there was no limit the length of the grieving process for the loss of a loved one. I believe that you will always suffer for that loss, but how you handle it becomes the story to follow.

Whereas that woman in the group chose to wallow in her grief, I chose not to. My choice was to find a silver lining in my black cloud, and try to understand that this happened for reasons unknown to me and will forever affect me. How I let it affect me becomes my choice. How I deal with it is another choice.

A young friend of mine once said- "pain is inevitable- suffering is optional"—Those wise words came from a 14-year-old terminally ill child. I've never forgotten them. Through the loss of my son, they became my mantra. It will always hurt knowing that he is not here with us. That pain will never go away, but I will do everything in my power to embrace it in a positive light and share that light with the world. I will continue to write in my journal until the day that the journal becomes the book.

A few years ago, my husband died. I did not know how to work the sprinkler system, where the extra light bulbs were kept, or even where the pressure cooker was!! I did know that I would get out of bed every morning and take a step forward every day.

Rose Bourassa

Many a night, my daughter and I discuss the "what ifs" of losing her brother and father. There are so many silver linings to be found in her brother's death. We have even found a silver lining or three in her dad's death. Each one helps us deal with the hand we've been dealt.

There is no describing the pain of losing the two most influential men in your life. Knowing that they are together in the afterlife is comforting. Not knowing if my husband chastised our son for his departure is something I will have to wait to find out when I arrive there.

You never get over your grief; you learn to live through it. Each of us must find our path in dealing with grief. We will all grieve differently. One fact I am sure of is that I will not suffer in my misery. Grief has forever changed me. I will forever carry that hurt with me, but while I carry it, I will share the silver linings found along the way, hoping they may be of value to someone else who is suffering needlessly.

Rose Bourassa

The men in my life...

Blessed to have them to love and be loved by them.

Losing them both has forever changed me.

"I will hold you in my heart until I can hold you again in heaven."

Forever Changed

LEONA CARRIERE JOANNETTE

I, Léona, am a returning author with At Above And Beyond. Besides being a widow, I am also a mother, a grandmother, a great-grandmother and a retired school teacher. I wish to be remembered as someone who lives by her beliefs.

BELIEVE is a popular word found in my vocabulary.

Forever Changed

FOREVER CHANGED
BY LEONA CARRIERE JOANNETTE

Learn from Yesterday!
                        Live for Today!
                                          Hope for Tomorrow!

"Let Your Faith Be Bigger Than Your Fear 2023" was written on a journal received at Christmas time, presented by my granddaughter and her two lovely girls. This beautiful surprise gave me the drive to keep on writing.

In life, we inevitably have Ups and Downs. Three days before my wedding, on a Wednesday afternoon, I was sitting alone in the living room, making colourful flowers with facial tissues. Onto heart-shaped cardboard, I would paste these beauties. This was the fad at the time. On my special day, I would decorate the back of the car used to travel from home to church, to the photographer and to the hall for the meal, where numerous guests would be waiting. Finally, after hours of work, I tried to pick up and clear the leftover material. Suddenly, an excruciating pain went down my spine! Unable to straighten up, with no one around to help, I crawled on my knees to a bedroom close by, then onto the bed with the use of my hands. Can you imagine what went through my mind at the time, powerless and in great pain? As people arrived, they tried to help me but to no avail. No way I was getting up at supper time, or going upstairs to my room at night time. Eventually, the doctor was called in. Shots were administered and painkillers were taken. Doctor's orders: "Complete rest...no exertion!"

Léona Carrière Joannette

Putting my faith in God, by Friday night I managed to attend church practice for the wedding ceremony. On Saturday morning, what a disappointment, as torrential rain poured down and continued all day long. No decor on the car...Take out your umbrella...

Thanks to family members, especially my maid of honor, who happened to be my sister, things finally fell into place. Little did I know what would happen next. I thought I was strong enough to go through the ceremony but... I cried uncontrollably all the way through. Thanks to my father who handed me his handkerchief, I was able to wipe away the tears. So many ideas and questions going through my mind. "What will the priest and guests think of this behaviour?" "Oh no...my make-up for pictures?" Well, we made it to church, then to the photographer, and finally to the hall to greet our guests, in the pouring rain!!

During the evening, I was not allowed to do much. Please note: I love dancing...When the time came for the wedding dance, guess who intervened?

Right...my father! His heart was in a right place, but no way was I to miss this dance. We convinced him that it would be okay for just a little while. How long is a while? Five minutes, if that!! He really wanted me to walk out of the building on my own two feet. Happily, the wedding party took over. No way was I to move from my chair, not with a bodyguard at my side, and he was not my husband. LOL

Another downer that evening was when Rhéal and I presented ourselves in our hotel bedroom, and Surprise!!..

Léona Carrière Joannette

Someone was in our bed...Now for the KICKER...My doctor had suggested that no intimate time should occur for the next TWO weeks!!!

After our short honeymoon, there were doctor appointments, x-rays and tests taken. Unfortunately, I was told that before long I would be in a wheelchair. Being a school teacher and on my feet all day long aggravated my situation. Chiropractors became my savior. At times, I had to leave my classroom for emergency visits. Thanks to understanding principals and teachers who took over my classroom and drove me to the chiropractor. Often I was sent home to recuperate for a couple of days, weeks, or a leave of absence.

By Christmas of our first year of marriage, we were pregnant. How happy and excited we were until problems stepped in. Yes, my lower back and legs would not cooperate. Last resort, I needed to wear a corset, with metal supports and hooks to fasten, with additional strings for better support. This started at my chest and continued down past my thighs, which allowed me to teach until the end of May. It was used during the hot summer months and saved our beautiful daughters' life.

I went back to work at the end of October. Near the end of November, I came home drained. Our girl had a medical condition and was often in pain.

We had to take shifts during the night, in order to rest for our work in the morning. I worked in the next town and had to take the bus by 7h30 to make it on time. My husband left

Léona Carrière Joannette

earlier than me, so I was left to prepare our daughter for her transport to the babysitter a block away. Fortunately, my dad was working the night shift at the time. He would pick up my little angel on his way home, where my mom would care for her. They were a God-send.

One particular day, returning home, exhausted from work, I opened the screened door as a piece of paper fell to the ground. Picking it up I realized it was a picture of Jesus with a prayer entitled "Don't Quit." Sitting down from lack of energy, I read this uplifting message. Who brought this? Where did it come from? Of course, this was what I needed at that time in my life. This lifted my Spirits enormously. With mixed feelings, I wiped my tears, thanking the angel who left it on my doorstep.

A small gesture can make a big difference in one's life. Good actions give us strength and inspire good actions in others. What you do makes a difference. You have to decide what kind of difference you want to make. With a new day comes new strength and new thoughts. Because of this problem with my back, I realized that walking was the only remedy to prevent me from ending up in a wheelchair. So, an exercise I did, and still do daily, before getting up in the morning. Later, I began walking the hallways of my building, and using the stairs to bring me to all of its 8 floors. While doing this exercise, I pray for everyone in my residence, family and friends, including all of those in the world who are in need! I call this "SOUL TALK."

If you read my chapter in the book "Friendships...Bonds Between Souls", it will help you to understand the powerful

Léona Carrière Joannette

connection that exists between our Creator, Heavenly Spiritual Allies and myself. Without their help I would not be here today! I have learned that Spirituality helps in achieving Happiness.

Since the death of my husband in 2009, my routine has changed. He is closer to me today, more than ever, as he silently slipped further into my heart.

Now I rarely leave my bedroom without reciting my morning prayers, and sprinkling Holy water on a picture frame of Jesus and another of Marie. They are gifts inherited from my in-laws. They remind me of my mother-in-law who had both legs amputated because of the lack of circulation. Also, I have two statues from my grandparents on my dad's side, one of Jesus, and the other of Marie.

They were found abandoned in a closet wrapped in rags. While visiting, I saw them being taken out of their hiding place, for a Carrières' family reunion. What a pitiful state they were in. Thankfully nobody had claimed them, so I joyfully inherited them. With love, a lot of work was done to bring them to their originality. I was told that they were on my grand-maman Carrieres' side table when she passed away. She was diabetic and her legs were blackening. These remind me of her. My dad also diabetic, had one leg amputated, then later on the second one, where he succumbed to his illness. How they must have suffered! I value my legs very much, thanking God for the ability to keep on walking. These precious pictures and statues of Marie and Jesus, remind me of my ancestors who prayed in

Léona Carrière Joannette

their own way, as I did and still do during my periods of back pain.

As humans, sometimes we hold on to our problems by trying to solve them by ourselves. We don't look at the big picture, we forget the wisdom of letting go. This is not easily done, for these hardships can bring you down, and drained of energy. Scripture tells us to acknowledge our powerlessness and fully turn our problems over to God. To be able to do that we have to be willing to let go of them. It is then that God sends us the peace that surpasses all understanding and guides us through our crisis.
After fifty-eight years since my diagnosis, I am grateful and celebrate God's gift of life today. With all these beautiful souls in heaven, I make the most of God's gifts by walking the floors with a heavenly purpose. I learned that our Lord's power is working through our weaknesses.
Where there is Hope, there is Faith!
Where there is Faith, Miracles happen!!

BELIEVE!!!

Widowed for almost 14 years, I Believe that my husband never left me. He simply slid further down into my heart, where he resides to this day.

Léona Carrière Joannette

I BELIEVE:

-That people are GIFTS sent to us by GOD...

-In my Inner and Outer BEAUTY and STRENGTH...

-In turning my Problems over to GOD and learning to Let Go...

-In the STRENGTH of a Mother's LOVE...

-In achieving HAPPINESS through SPIRITUALITY...

-That HAPPINESS lies WITHIN...

-In letting my FAITH be bigger than my FEARS...

-That with FAITH...MIRACLES happen!

ANNE JOANNETTE-WHITE

Anne enjoys discovering her truest self. She recognizes her roles as an emotional being, a mother, an author, a daughter, a teacher, a trusted friend, a spiritual healer, a student, a wife and as an empath. These describe who she is as a leader.

Anne continues living life with gratitude. She is grateful for all of the opportunities to show love and to be loved. Also, she is grateful for all of life's challenges that help her grow, learn and heal. This chapter is dedicated to all who have felt alone and empty in their loss. May you feel my light of hope for healing.

THE GIFT OF ETERNAL LOVE
BY ANNE JOANNETTE-WHITE

Looking back on my life experiences, I remember feeling many types of grief
-needing to be a perfect daughter and student
-feelings of being excluded
-learning to understand and manage my feelings after the death of close family members, friends and pets
-living with fear and anxiety
-living with not knowing the reasons "why"
-feelings of not being good enough or unworthy

I learned to live with these griefs. Their purpose was to teach me something about myself because they were my life lessons, right? None of these types of grief compared to the painful ordeal I experienced on May 6th, 1998. The day I changed forever.

I started the day full of hope and positivity. I was already maman to a thoughtful and tender-hearted 18-month-old and expecting my second child. It was unbelievable how quickly and deeply connected I felt with this baby. I already loved him so so much. (Yes, I absolutely knew it was a boy and I had already named him Neil Maxime.) However, by the end of *that* day, I remember feeling numb, empty and alone. I was curled up in a fetal position in bed feeling like I did something wrong. *It* was my fault. I suffered a miscarriage at approximately 6 weeks of pregnancy. My baby was the size of a pea.

Anne Joannette-White

My OBGYN tried comforting me by saying *It* wasn't my fault and I didn't do anything wrong...things like this just happen, it's common.

"It's common Anne, snap out of it," I used to tell myself. I miscarried during the first trimester, therefore, if it's going to happen, well that's the best time to do so. *The best time* -so, why am I so sad? I should be grateful, right? I felt incapable of feeling what was normal to feel because I felt unworthy to grieve; my pain wasn't as important as other sadder circumstances. I "should" feel lucky. I didn't experience a miscarriage in the last trimester, or after hearing the baby's heartbeat, or a stillbirth, or even losing the baby a few hours after giving birth. Those were the thoughts that made me bury my grief and pain of losing my baby so soon in the pregnancy.

"Snap out of it Anne"...I continued telling myself. I had a beautiful daughter who didn't understand why maman was sad, crying and didn't want to play with her. My husband did his best to take care of her while I rested. He took it upon himself to do what I couldn't; he broke the news to our family and friends. I felt so bad for him. "Thank you, it's appreciated!" What does one say upon hearing that kind of news and what do you say in return? We were both in survival mode. My husband didn't know what to say to me to help me feel better. He honestly tried and I loved him for that. Yet, "*it*" happened to me, to my physical, spiritual and emotional bodies. We lived with the compensating thought "at least we have our daughter," since she was our true ray of sunshine. I didn't realize that I was pushing further down into my grief. I decided to go back to work a few days later and even celebrated Mother's Day to help my loved ones feel better around me. I worked hard to try to forget *"it"*. I had to be the maman and wife my daughter and husband needed me to be.

Life continued for us. A few months later, we received the confirmation that we were expecting again. It was so difficult to keep that secret to ourselves, but we chose to wait after the first trimester, just in case. What a pleasure and a relief to announce the fantastic news that I was pregnant again. My sadness and emotional pain from the miscarriage were pushed further down. Nevertheless, eleven months after the miscarriage, a second beautiful and healthy daughter was born. I was truly happy and grateful. My family was complete.

A few years later, I treated myself to my first Reiki energy healing session. What an amazing first experience. My practitioner held her hands over my body and started asking me questions regarding my son. My *son*? In that instant, memories of my miscarriage came flooding back. I started crying without understanding why...all the years of sadness, guilt and emptiness that I pushed back were all coming to the surface. I will always be grateful to my chosen Reiki practitioner for helping me observe and understand my emotions. My healer was also a gifted medium and she proceeded to describe this little boy's soul that was in the room beside me, my son. We shared time together in this physical world for a precious 6 weeks but his true role was being my spiritual guide. This moment is when true healing started for me. I do feel his energy and his love. I was spiritually connected to him. I walked away from that session feeling renewed, lighter and feeling new love for myself. I truly felt a new chapter was starting, the healing chapter.

Gratefulness replaced my sorrow. Eternal love replaced my feelings of loneliness and of guilt. I feel connected and understand the reason for this grief experience. The healing continues for me and this gift has helped open many other doors in the Spiritual and energy healing fields. I am learning the meaning of living an authentic life. I am learning not to dismiss my emotions and TRUST that "this too shall pass." I still feel my son's spirit visiting me from time to time to give me a reassuring hug or a good nudge when I let fear take over my thoughts. I am appreciating this special bond. Since "my Michael's" due date was around Christmas time, I have been allowing myself to sit with my grief of his loss. Every Christmas, I remember the time we had "together" in this lifetime. I ask his soul to shine his loving light on me while I continue to share my healing light with others I meet on this adventure called life on Earth.

I am forever changed for the better.

It hurts because it matters
John Green

Sometimes the smallest things, take up the most room in our heart.
A.A.Milne

How lucky I am to have something that makes saying goodbye so hard.
Winnie the Pooh

Grieving is like broken ribs. On the outside you look fine, but with every breath it hurts.
Unknown

You didn't stay for long, but in those precious weeks, you changed me forever.
Zoe Clark Coates

CINDY MALLORY

Cindy Mallory is a yoga teacher, reiki master and writer. She is on a lifelong healing journey and is inspired by the words of Maya Angelou, "there is no greater agony than bearing an untold story inside of you." She hopes that through finding her voice and living her truth, she can help light the way for others to find their path to healing. You can reach her at cindy.mallory@utoronto.ca
* It's OK That You're Not OK ~ by Megan Devine

A JOURNEY OF LOVE
BY CINDY MALLORY

Grief is a state of grace, the outcome of having loved deeply.
Mountains cannot be surmounted except by winding paths – von Goethe

It was midnight on New Year's Eve, just over a year since the death of my husband. Fireworks from the nearby village woke me with a start. A sense of panic overwhelmed me and I couldn't breathe. I suddenly had a feeling in my gut that big things would happen this year, and I'd have no control over any of it. It felt like a fast-flowing river and I'd have no choice but to jump in.

Terrified, I began to sob, shaking uncontrollably. Whatever would happen in the coming year would be without Doug. I felt like I was on the edge of a cliff, looking at an unknown land. I would be walking without him, creating a life without him. Last New Year's Eve I'd still been in shock. This year I was aware.

This was me being pushed to choose to live. Yet I had no choice at all. It was like an invisible hand was pushing me, showing me that how I'd been living wasn't sustainable. I was slowly killing myself.

Up until now, I'd just been surviving, one day at a time, still reeling from the feeling that the unthinkable was real. Many days it was all I could do to brush my teeth. Nutrition was a concept from another life. Vegetables found their way to my fridge only to die. My blood pressure and arthritis were keeping me crippled, and many days I crawled up the stairs and hobbled around the house. At 65, I felt like I had imagined 90 would feel like. I'd had pneumonia twice in a few months and most days didn't feel well. I did my best to put on a brave face for the world. I wondered if something was wrong with me. My broken heart was far from healed.

The reality is our culture has it wrong. Healing doesn't happen in a specific timeframe, or in any kind of order. Grief has its own path, and every journey is different. Grief is the boss and the only way to heal is to surrender to it, from one day to the next. There is no going around it, only through.

I found that my life had become a dance between four ways of being; resting, active mourning, nurturing future plans; and living in the present. This dance is what gives space for profound healing to occur.

Resting: In the early months rest and active mourning took up most of my days. Rest meant I couldn't do anything except surrender to complete despair and exhaustion. It was a time of being unable to fully face the depth of the trauma of his death. It was simply too big. It was a way of acknowledging just how sad I was and letting myself be in it. I comforted myself the best I could, moving slowly through daily life. The resting allowed my body and spirit to make room for more healing and to slowly accept this new reality.

Cindy Mallory

Active mourning: In order to avoid getting lost in negative patterns, active mourning has been crucial. This means facing the sharp edges of my grief. Sometimes I have to push myself, but it keeps me from getting stuck. I write out my feelings and this always leads to a deep dive into my deepest pain. Although crying doesn't change anything, it frees up space inside and shifts how I feel. I also share my feelings with people I love, have seen a grief counsellor, and joined a grief group. I go for the same long drives we used to do together and sit in our favorite places.

Last summer I learned to ride his motorcycle, and that helped me feel close to him while riding.

Sometimes I just sit in his chair holding one blanket of his that I can't wash.

Active mourning is so very necessary to my healing. It makes it real. It's a message to myself that how I feel matters. Although less frequent as time goes by, this grief work is vital to my health, well-being and ability to move forward in life. It is the fire that ignites profound inner growth and change.

Nurturing the Future: Losing a life partner means the path we were on is forever altered. For me, it was shattered. An author from a book on grief* who had recently lost her husband, said it was "like standing in blinking horror, on the edge of the gaping hole that used to be her life." Recreating my life means digging deep to find out who I am, and exploring possibilities for a new future. In the early months, I would try to take a step forward, only to fall back down again through illness or despair. Yet making plans meant part of me believed there would be a future.

It was after the first year that looking ahead really became possible. Threads of future ideas started to hold a tiny bit of hope, even excitement. These rays of light were still fleeting and interrupted by rest and active mourning. Yet the energy in them was gaining momentum, and I felt the pull to surrender. A voice inside was telling me that if I choose to believe in myself and take a leap of faith, the bridge will be there.

Living in the present moment – gratitude: Like 'nurturing the future' this part wasn't available to me in the first year. When I first found myself feeling peaceful and enjoying being in the present, it came as a shock. And I felt a little guilty. How could I feel okay when he was gone?

Yet my answer was that he would be cheering to see me doing well. It was all he would have wanted. Although bits of gratitude had already been threaded through every day, once I was able to sink into the moment and look around, it truly grabbed hold of me. I was beginning to rejoin the living. On the wings of my healing, gratitude opens my heart to life.

Together these ways of being have been the framework for surviving what feels impossible.
With this loss death had come right up to me and I saw its immensity. I looked upon its face, knowing I had no control. It took him without apology. It felt like part of me had died too, and I had a foot in both sides. Sometimes I feel the

Cindy Mallory

beauty of the other side leaking through, especially when I receive messages from Doug through serendipitous events that feel magical.

They shock me, comfort me, and help to strengthen what I have always known. That the world is far more magnificent than anything we can imagine. This grief, more than any other, has opened a window to my soul.

On this journey of healing, I learned that love doesn't end. Instead, it is magnified and surrounds me like an energy field. Although it is impossible to be aware of it all the time, when I feel its magnitude, the fullness and grace of it cracks open my heart and it feels like a miracle.

In the wake of profound loss, we are gutted, brokenhearted, and sometimes broken, yet still, the beauty and resilience of the human spirit shines through. We find a way to bear it. We surrender, we learn, we fall and get up again. We recreate ourselves. We keep assimilating our grief, piece by piece, day by day, until we are able to answer the call to live again. We are always forever changed.

"When you come out of the storm you won't be the same person that walked in" – Haruki Murakani

TAMMY BRAZEAU

Tammy, is a daughter, wife, stepmother and grandmother. She is a full-time support worker. She enjoys journaling, and also enjoys travelling and spending time with family and friends. She is a fun-loving caring individual.

This is Tammy's second time being published in a collaborative book.

She welcomes you to connect with her
Tammybrazo@gmailcom

LOVE IS GREATER THAN PAIN
BY TAMMY BRAZEAU

Most of us relate grieving to someone we have lost. Ever wonder what it feels like to live with living grief?

Lisa, a loving mother, stepmother and grandmother, is also a caring loving wife who suffers from living grief. You see, her husband suffers from Parkinson's and Dementia. There was a moment when she realized that he was no longer the same person. Life had changed and the 'him' before slowly faded into the fabric of the years past. If she looked closely, the scars were there but they no longer caused pain. Now they were simply a part of her story.

"Instead of running away, I ran to him. That became something that created the strength in who I am."

Mourning the living is painful, complicated, overwhelming and handled differently by each person. We typically relate grief with funerals or sympathy cards. It is possible to mourn the loss of someone still very much alive.

Their Story.

They met in January 1996 at a singles dance. He was the nicest, most handsome man in the crowd. He treated her like royalty, the way she deserved. They had a few really good years of love, laughter and adventure. They were

Tammy Brazeau

pretty much perfect. Then in 2007, things started happening. He was having occasional tremors, and then a few more symptoms that were concerning. He was diagnosed shortly thereafter with Parkinson's disease.

It has been a struggle to see the man she loves deeply, slowly change and soon after watching him lose his independence as well. Every day some new symptom would appear. Some were small changes, and then the big ones would happen fast. How would she cope with this?

With love, that is all she could do, love him with everything she had. Adore him. Praise him on good days, and enjoy every moment, because the reality is now, they have become special moments. Very sad, but a huge reality shift for her. Loving him unconditionally became the only way!

Tammy Brazeau

No matter where life leads you, be good and be grateful to the people around you. Every single person has been strategically placed in your life for a reason. Perhaps they are here to help you along. To strengthen your courage or come to grips with you being able to feel your emotions. Whatever it may be, even if only for a moment, you can be certain that there is a reason.

One of the hardest parts of grieving someone who is still here is that you are forced to accept a changed relationship that you don't want.

Grief is often referred to as an emotional reaction to the loss of someone or something important. Grieving someone who is alive but not necessarily present introduces a host of unexpected challenges. You might be forced into unfamiliar roles, such as becoming a full-time caregiver.

Sometimes, it may be hard to stay hopeful, or you can feel lost without a good support system. There may be no words that can help you, but someone just listening can be the greatest support.

A grieving person must resolve the emotional and life changes that come with the death, or the possibility of losing a loved one. What if your loved one is still alive, but no longer the same person because of an illness?

When a loved one develops a serious illness it's normal to go through an emotional experience.

Tammy Brazeau

Time seems to freeze when you learn that someone you love has a serious illness like Dementia.

The fears and feelings that surface now are better aired than ignored. The fear that your loved one has lost his independence, and security and has impaired abilities, can cause the future to become unknown and scary.

The sadness and the questions about what happens now, begin. How do we cope with this? The feeling of sorrow, anger, depression and denial surface. How to accept this? Although not everyone experiences this, these feelings are normal, and it is important to talk with your family, friends and others for support.

Keeping a journal, the process of writing down your thoughts, is a beneficial way to reduce your stress and anxiety. It allows you to clear your mind.

Now, the time is near to possibly consider some help. Home care programs are available to relieve the caregiver. It is so important that the caregiver accepts the help. It relieves them from day-to-day activities such as personal hygiene and incontinence care. It is important to accept care, as it promotes and maintains your health by reducing your stress levels. Accepting help can be a struggle at times. Knowing that you are burning out, or about to. Having someone come in and help your loved one is ensuring the pressure is taken off of you.

Tammy Brazeau

Succeeding as a spousal caregiver means knowing when to ask for help. It's important to find time for yourself and to make peace with your partner.

Many caregivers throw themselves into their new roles so wholeheartedly that they neglect their own care. So, support from family and friends becomes vitally important. If you keep a lot of information private, people will have no idea how bad it might be behind closed doors, and they won't be able to help you.

Today, my mom and her husband still love each other deeply. They enjoy sitting outside on the porch on a sunny day, or watching a hockey game cheering for their favorite teams. Some days are good, and some days are harder than others.

She still cares for him at home. She has daily struggles as you can imagine, they both do. The saddest part, to me, is that he might not remember who she is one day, his loving wife, his caregiver, his best friend and soulmate.

Tammy Brazeau

To My Mother, My Hero...

Be proud of how you've been handling these past years. The silent battles you have fought in the moments where you had to humble yourself, as you wiped your own tears.

Pat yourself on the back!!

Celebrate your strength!!

You're an amazing, strong woman!!

My mother Lisa, and my stepfather Godfroy xoxo

Wherever You Will Go ~ Lyrics by The Calling

So lately, been wondering
Who will be there to take my place
When I'm gone, you'll need love
To light the shadows on your face
If a great wave shall fall
And fall upon us all
Then between the sand and stone
Could you make it on your own?
If I could, then I would
I'll go wherever you will go
Way up high or down low
I'll go wherever you will go
And maybe, I'll find out
A way to make it back someday
To watch you, to guide you
Through the darkest of your days
If a great wave shall fall
And fall upon us all
Well then I hope there's someone out there
Who can bring me back to you
If I could, then I would
I'll go wherever you will go
Way up high or down low
I'll go wherever you will go
Run away with my heart
Run away with my hope
Run away with my love

NATASHA ANNE BOULANGER

Hello readers, my name is Natasha Boulanger. I enjoy being outdoors. Nature is my calling, and I love the smell of fresh air. Connecting to nature through fishing, hunting, and walks in the good outdoors is my favourite thing to do. I am in my early thirties, married, and have two beautiful girls. My home is full of pets too. I consider myself a crazy animal lover. This is my fourth time writing in a collective book. I am overjoyed to be able to share my stories and to connect with others.

PEBBLES
BY NATASHA ANNE BOULANGER

Grief can take on many forms. For some, grief is caused by the loss of a loved one. For others, it is triggered by the absence of something they longed to have. This chapter tells the story of a young girl, one I knew very well. It will shed light on her grief, as she grieved throughout a very big part of her life. She grieved for her childhood, and this grief shaped her life's path. This girl grieved the absence of a proper childhood; some might even say she grieved the childhood that was robbed from her. Readers might find this story a tad horrifying, and some might be able to relate. My goal for sharing this young girl's story is to let others, who may have been through something similar, know that they are NOT alone. It is important to go through a grieving period when your life is changed dramatically, or traumatically. However, it is also important to remember that there is ALWAYS a better and brighter future if you commit to the work of healing, and never give up. Keep looking forward and never backward.

Pebbles' parents split when she was just shy of two years of age. Her father had primary custody of her and her older sibling. She has no memory of her parents as a couple. Her father had remarried a young woman and they later had a beautiful child together. Things in Pebbles's life were not all that bad in the beginning. However, when she was six years old, things started to come down on her like a bad storm. A storm that lasted for years and caused a great deal of pain. Pebbles's stepmother played an important role in her life. She treated Pebbles like her own and cared for her deeply. Unfortunately, things did not work out between Pebbles's father and her stepmother, so they decided to part ways. The sudden departure of her stepmother was Pebbles's second experience with grief. She was much too young to understand why her stepmother was no longer a part of her life, but that did not stop her from hoping life would throw better days her way.

Pebbles was thrilled when her father met another woman that had three children of her own. She was excited to have more siblings and to be in a loving blended family. The relationship grew quickly. They moved in together in less than a year. Pebbles's new stepmother took on her new role fast and did not hold back from manipulating Pebbles, Pebbles's older sibling, nor her father. One can never truly see someone for who they really are until they have the opportunity to live in the same home as them.

Readers, have you ever watched the Disney princess movies Cinderella and Rapunzel? Pebbles could easily relate to these princesses. She was deprived of affection, empathy, and basic needs. Her stepmother often withheld food. Pebbles had to sneak food, or rely on the younger children to sneak some for her. She was forced to care for the younger children and to complete household chores that are typically reserved for adults. When she wasn't doing either of these things, Pebbles was, at first, confined to her room, then to her bed. She spent a great deal of time staring at her bedroom ceiling and walls. So much so, that she began to count the cracks in the walls and the framing nails that she could see through the plaster and paint.

Today, she could likely still tell you how many of these items she counted. Pebbles's father was frequently away for work and was mostly absent when Pebbles was mistreated. Pebbles lost her self-worth, self-confidence, and self-love when she was seven years old. At seven years old, Pebbles was sexually assaulted. She was told to keep quiet and manipulated to think that no one would believe her. The sexual abuse became more frequent, happening almost daily until she turned twelve. She trained her brain to block out the sounds, sights and smells throughout each assault. She felt empty.

Apart from daily sexual abuse, Pebbles was constantly called names by her stepmother. She was often told: "You will get nowhere in life. You're as dumb as a doorknob… keep dreaming."

She also experienced physical abuse and humiliation. Her face was smacked, her hair pulled, and she was poorly nourished. Pebbles remembers when her stepmother chopped off her hair, leaving only an inch or two of hair. She was nine years old. Pebbles knew this was not normal.

She craved longer school hours every day because she dreaded returning home where she felt so unloved. The compilation of abandonment, sexual abuse, physical abuse, emotional abuse, and neglect took a toll on her mental health and on her self-esteem. She struggled to make friends and was bullied at school, but she felt that it was easier to deal with school problems than with those she faced at home. Her grades were also terrible, but she did not understand why her learning skills were so poor. She felt like a robot, living not for herself, but simply existing for others even though they treated her with such disrespect. She was blamed for her flaws, and told to "grow up" and "get it together." But, she was just a child! The people she trusted and loved the most in her life mistreated her and let her down countless times. However, Pebbles remained hopeful of a bigger and brighter future. She knew that one day, she would break free like the princesses did in the movies. Disney was her comfort. Hearing the words of Disney movies gave her hope that her dreams would come true, one day. She committed to never giving up and kept looking for the positives in life.

The constant state of fight or flight that Pebbles experienced throughout her life took an unimaginable toll on her mental well-being. Ever since she could remember, she would wish upon her birthday candles, or a shooting star, to be happy, loved, and accepted.

Unravelling the effects of abuse means unlearning the defence mechanisms and survival tactics it creates. This is challenging because they are so deeply embedded in one self that they are often attributed to identity and personality. However, that it NOT who Pebbles is. The abuse she experienced should not define her. Trauma makes people tolerate a lot of shit that they don't deserve. Pain builds walls, but healing creates doors. Pebbles worked hard and focused on healing because she feared losing the people she had built relationships with, those who genuinely cared about her. Traumatized children often dream of someone coming to rescue them…they never imagine it being themselves as an adult.

Natasha Anne Boulanger

Now, after reading this young girl's story, you are likely wondering how I know Pebbles. I am Pebbles. I am happy to have overcome the barriers I faced in my life. My traumatic past does not define me it only makes me stronger. I learned so much while healing, and hope to continue learning because self-worth and self-love are not destinations, but part of my journey. There are so many possible roads to go down; left turns, right turns, U-turns. We have the entire map right in front of us. We will reach a time in our life when we have limited U-turns, a bunch of closed roads, and the majority of paths are in our rearview mirror. There is no turning back; we are forced to focus on the present and our future.

I am blessed with some very good and supportive people in my life. Many of whom have helped me out of physically and emotionally harmful situations. This overprotective mother was once an under protected child. Read the last sentence again... I know I had to read it a few times, and wow it's a real feel. It's strange to reflect on my past and to recognize my own growth. I now have my own beautiful family and I am married to my prince charming. I am proud of where I stand today and of all the work I have put in myself. If you have ever been through something similar you are NOT alone, and you ARE allowed to grieve. Grief is part of our healing journey. Just remember things do get better.

Natasha Anne Boulanger

Here are some of my favourite Disney quotes that made a lasting impression on me:

"Oh yes, the past can hurt,
but the way I see it, you can either run
from it or learn from it."
-Rafiki

"The flower that blooms in adversity
Is the most rare and beautiful of all."
-Mulan

"Just keep swimming, just keep swimming"
-Finding Nemo

"If you focus on what's left behind,
you will never see what lies ahead."
-Gusteau (Ratatouille)

"Always let your conscience be your guide."
-Jiminy cricket

"First, Think.
Second,
Believe.
Third,
Dream.
And finally, dare."
-Disney

> "And at last I see the light,
> it's like the fog has lifted and it's like the sky is new"
> -Rapunzel

> "No matter how your heart is grieving,
> If you keep on believing, the dream that you wish
> will come true."
> -Cinderella

Grief moves through the body, it inhabits it, it becomes part of the skin, the cells, and it makes a home there, a permanent home. However, you learn to live with it and to grow in spite of it. You will be happy again; never in the same way as before, but that is the point of growth. You always find a way toward happiness. I chose to uplift myself, to keep looking and moving forward. Will you let your grief drown you, or will you face it and come out stronger on the other side? Be brave, and be strong, but never forget that it is ok to grieve.

Natasha Anne Boulanger

Forever Changed

"YOU CAN RECOGNIZE SURVIVORS OF ABUSE BY THEIR COURAGE. WHEN SILENCE IS SO VERY INVITING, THEY STEP FORWARD AND SHARE THEIR TRUTH SO OTHERS KNOW THEY AREN'T ALONE."

— JEANNE MCELVANEY, <u>HEALING INSIGHTS: EFFECTS OF ABUSE FOR ADULTS ABUSED AS CHILDREN</u>

DORIS ARTNER

Meet Doris Artner, owner and founder of Heal Thy Self Reiki & Wellness. A dedicated and passionate healer who has always sought happiness and healing for herself and others. As an Intuitive Empath, Reiki Master, Certified Emotional Freedom Technique Practitioner and Chakra Healer, Sound Therapist, Aromatherapist, Tarot reader and Author, she brings a wealth of knowledge and experience to her practice. Doris is a firm believer that every person is in control of their own healing journey and is committed to helping individuals along their path to healing. With Doris's compassionate guidance and gentle healing touch, you can begin your own journey toward happiness, health and fulfillment.

FROM GRIEF TO EMPOWERMENT
BY DORIS ARTNER

At the tender age of three, my life was forever changed when my parents decided to separate. A time of critical development for a child forming emotional attachments toward parental figures. Unbeknownst to me at the time, this marked the beginning of my abandonment difficulties. Through the years, this issue would reveal its ugly head over and over in my life, especially within my relationships. Three years later, my parents reunited and once again we became a family unit, living out our years, until a day I remember vividly! We listened intently as the doctor explained in the hospital emergency room that my father had only a few weeks to live. He had been diagnosed with stage four lung cancer, which had caused his limiting breath. I felt an overwhelming sense of nausea immediately. I had gone into shock! The thought of my dad not being a part of my life was too much to handle. Even when my parents had gone on vacation to Austria in the past, I had hugged my dad so tightly, while tears ran down my cheeks, as they were leaving to board the plane, the feeling of abandonment resurfaced.

It was August 23rd, 2014. The tragedy was felt across my entire family. Although knowing the death of my father was coming, the actual day was never truly prepared for. He passed away very quickly within 3 weeks of his diagnosis. In the Palliative Care unit at the hospital, it was my turn to stay the night with my dad. My sister and I were taking turns and tonight was my first night. Much to my surprise, my sister had planned on staying the night too. I was extremely relieved and felt the heaviness in my chest lift. As it was getting late, my mom, son, niece and close family friends had just left for the day. Only a few family members had stayed a while longer. I am actually tearing up at the memory of what happened next, partly feeling the sadness but mostly because of how beautiful the event was. Due to limited breathing, it was easiest for my dad to be propped up or to sit up altogether. We sat him up. My sister and I at either side of him. We held him in between us and within a few short moments we both knew that this was it. It was time!

We looked at each other and I stated clearly, "Let's do this!" She nodded in agreement. We knew what was coming but remained calm and ready. My sister, with her eyes closed at his right. My eyes open, watching his breath in his oxygen mask, on his left. The nurses and the few family members that remained were still and quiet as they watched, like they weren't even there. I continued to speak, now only to my dad, knowing he couldn't verbally respond.

"It's ok daddy, go toward the Light," I could feel his hesitancy.

"We're going to be ok," I continued. He reached his arms out briefly. "They're waiting for you." I knew his parents were waiting for him. I could see the calm on his face, I knew his time was close.

"We love you, daddy." "Bye, daddy."

Doris Artner

My sister had walked our dad, hand in hand to the Veil. When his time had come, he had turned to look at her, smiled and continued through. I watched him take his last breath. There was an unfamiliar but peaceful stillness. Together, with so much love, we spiritually and physically led him Home. My sister and I looked at each other, tears welling up in our eyes, smiles forming as we just experienced the most amazing moment of our lives.

"We did It," were the only words I could say. The tears streamed down our cheeks. There was a sense of awe in the eyes of the nurses and family who had just witnessed such unforgettable beauty. We knew from this day forward that our lives were forever changed!

After his funeral, I was overwhelmed with grief. My father's death had once again stirred up feelings of abandonment within me. I wanted to die myself. Yet somehow, I knew my dad continued to be with me, in Spirit.

Doesn't it always seem that a life-changing event is what brings you to realizations you hadn't noticed before? The passing of my dad changed me. I began to see my life in a different light.

I realized there were problems in my marriage. My husband was not emotionally available to me, especially when I needed him the most. I also yearned to be ME! My true, authentic self but felt I couldn't do that in my marriage. I realized I had to be, whom I was expected to be. Crazy is who I was to my partner when I had spoken of spirituality, energy work or anything of the sort. I had been shut down, as it was unheard of had I even remotely mentioned intuition.

One day, while working at a retail store, a customer whom I hadn't seen before, asked me about a product. The conversation moved to her revealing how she was in an unhappy marriage, wanting to have left her husband years ago, but choosing to stay anyway. I smiled as I immediately recognized her as an 'Earth Angel', sent to guide me and give me a message. This conversation helped me make my decision about my own marriage and start a journey of self-discovery.

After my father's passing, I began counselling and continued attending regular Reiki treatments for help. Both played a significant role in my journey. They empowered me to learn more about healing myself, growing love for myself from within and gaining self-worth. Through healing, I was able to learn more about who I really am and deeply connect with my spirituality. I began to delve into meditation, aromatherapy, intuition, tarot and everything self-awareness. Reiki empowered me to finally leave an unhappy marriage. With Spirit's gentle push and through studying the art of Reiki energy healing, I become a catalyst to assist others on their own path to discover their truth and also to live a life of authenticity.

Although the passing of my father was heartbreaking, it brought me to a place of ongoing self-discovery and genuine happiness. I am overcoming my abandonment fears and learning to be true to myself. This journey hasn't been easy, but it has brought me a place of peace and

Doris Artner

understanding. I am forever grateful for the time I had with my dad. I know he will always be with me and continue to guide me, along my path toward truth, love and my Self.

SUSAN DIANE

I believe that most of the time most people make their greatest contribution and largest impact one person at a time, yet through my writing I hope to have a positive influence in a wider circle. In contrast to my working career as a graduate engineer and chartered professional accountant providing tax-related services, I am currently honouring a lifelong love of literature. In my first novel three voices spanning successive generations, recount a tale of extraordinary, because aren't we all in our own unique way, twentieth-century women? Consistent with my inclination to support individuals with personal money management, I provide life coaching, with an emphasis on wealth health and financial fitness.

You may contact me at thestoryteller@susandiane.ca

SERENDIPITY'S REMAINDER
BY SUSAN DIANE

The young woman's fingertips stroke the soft supple satin of the dress. The fabric is the pale blue hue of an early morning summer sky. It is the dress she wore at her bridal shower. It might have served as her wedding frock until she found a more elegant garment for the important day. She is sad she will never wear the glamorous gown of white taffeta embroidered with seed pearls and wisps of delicate lace. No help for it, she is resolved that there will be no wedding. She is done struggling; it has been a year of frustration. It should be her day and her vision. Every idea and detail is interrupted or disrupted. If Ted stood up to his mother and simply told her to butt out, it could be different, but he is mute and she herself has said too little. Her hopes are in chaos.

As she sits alone in her childhood bedroom, she pictures the stylish wedding that would never be celebrated in the beautiful banquet ballroom of the heritage waterfront venue. Chiffon curtains billow in the early evening breeze, the air moist with mist from the waves against the harbour breakwater. She imagines herself beside Ted, as they move slowly to the center of the room, hand in hand, towards a head table laid with gold-rimmed white china and sparkling crystal goblets of white wine. The floral arrangements are bright and strong, the ambers and oranges of autumn, all around is cream and light. Reality returns and she sits silent and sad, alone on her narrow single bed. She sits, not yet unpacked, but ready and determined to start over.

Susan Diane

For the past eight years, she has lived with her boyfriend, Ted, sharing a generous basement suite in his parent's house. When they decided to be married, they had put a deposit on a small condominium apartment, not yet constructed, it should have been ready soon after the wedding. The completion of the condominium has been delayed for another year and when it is done it will not be any part of her future. The loss of her dreams tortures her waking thoughts and torments her few precious sleeping hours. The man she loves did not stand at her side, and partnered with her against his family; it would have been worse after the exchange of their vows. She has walked away from a future with a meddlesome and maddening mother-in-law, the woman was out of control and her son was unable to defend his bride-to-be. It foreshadowed a miserable marriage.

It is good to be home with her parents and her maternal grandmother. Since her grandfather's recent death, her Nanna has been living with the young woman's parents. All the bedrooms in her family home are full and there is no empty place at their cozy kitchen table. Her dad loves to cook, and on holidays and for special occasions he dons his very big apron, to baste the turkey or brown the beef roast, creating a fabulous feast. Every other day of the year the kitchen is his undisputed domain, a big win for his family, he is a capable and creative cook. In this and so many other ways her dad looks after everyone, except himself. Now that she is at home, perhaps she can find opportunities to take care of him. She has missed her dad, and she is glad to see him every day, not just on infrequent weekends.

Susan Diane

*****

The young woman's father is pensive as he prepares dinner on his daughter's first evening home. His thoughts are conflicted; he likes Ted, but he is overjoyed to have his only child home again. She inhabits a special place in his heart, they share a cherished bond. Earlier, during the forty-five-minute drive to collect her and her belongings, as he maneuvered through the afternoon traffic on the busy highway, he had recalled fondly how every summer he and his daughter would visit with his parents, just the two of them. She was little then, and to make the long drive endurable, they would visit their favourite rest stops, for ice cream at one, for hamburgers and fresh-cut fries at the next.

Once at his parents', he would take his two best girls, his mother and his daughter, shopping. Infrequently, his mother bought some little thing for her precious only grandchild, but mostly they just wandered about the many shops chatting and laughing as they paused to examine possible purchases, while he sat watching their progress from the benches in the centre of the mall's hallway.

On the hottest afternoons, they swam in the cold water of Ramsey Lake. Six feet six inches tall, he was a human diving tower, lifting his little girl overhead, giggling she would jump from his shoulders, again and again, each time trusting he would be waiting when she surfaced.

After dinner, while they watched television, they would share a big bowl of hot buttery popcorn. Their favourite

Susan Diane

shows were Jeopardy and Hollywood Squares, his daughter delighted as her father and grandmother got all the answers. With game show genius, combining their knowledge of trivia, they could answer almost every question. He misses his own mother; she has been dead now for almost ten years. It is a loss he has never accepted. It will be nice to have his daughter home and share her daily routine. His mood is light, grateful for the turn of events. For his only child, in his usual way, he is eager to provide comfort and assistance; whatever is required.

*****

Outside of the shelter of her parents' home, at work and on weekends, she searches out new people to consume her attention and ease the emptiness she feels. Ten years is a long time with one partner. Tonight, she is in a crowded bar with her best girlfriend. She scans the nameless faces for another random stranger in the long succession of unsatisfying individuals she has met during the lonely months of winter, spring and now summer. Her attempts to find solace for her sadness are futile, temporary.

*****

It is almost a year since her decision to end her relationship with Ted. With some reservation she agrees to see him again; they go out on a date, to dinner and a movie. He picks her up from, and brings her back to, her parent's house. The evening is pleasant, and they establish a routine over the final weeks of the summer and into the fall. As the completion of the condominium is approaching, he asks her, would she consider moving into the apartment with him when it is ready.

"Maybe?" is her hesitant response. "It might work out, in a place of our own."

Silently she wonders, in their own home, would they be far enough away from his mother and her strong influence?

Her own parents support the new direction. They are very aware of how unhappy she is apart from him.

She moves into the shiny new compact condominium apartment with him just before Christmas. Over the holidays they split their time between her parents and his, his mother seems to be making a special effort to respect her son's independence. It is a happy Christmas, and the future is full of promise. Grateful she spent this year at home with her father and mother, she is optimistic that this time apart has strengthened her relationship with Ted and his family.

*****

In the new year her father is more tired than what they have come to expect. For thirty years he has worked the twelve-hour night shift at the local auto assembly plant; a choice that allowed him to share his daughter's daylight hours. He can barely breathe. His worn tan complexion, once warm with auburn undertones, is fading to a greyish pallor. She and her mother insist he seek medical advice.

Susan Diane

With his towering stature, he is a gentle giant; he has a huge heart, kind and caring, but it isn't strong, and it is sadly unsuitable to sustain his exceptional size when the cancer invades his lungs. Despite all efforts at optimism and positive thinking the inevitable comes quickly; time is limited.

For her parent's thirtieth wedding anniversary, celebrated around her father's hospital bed, she presents her prettily wrapped gift. Her father removes the bright multi coloured bow and peers into the blue and gold gift bag. She has joked about giving her dad a reason to stay with them but never imagined their efforts could be so quickly rewarded. Beneath the pale blue tissue, there is a positive pregnancy stick. The man weeps without reservation, tears of joy flow freely, he has never been so happy. He is complete, his beautiful daughter is settled with her partner. His first grandchild will be born in only a few months time. They all regard him with such expectation, he sees the naked hope in their expressions, the silent plea that he will wait for the baby's arrival.

He does not have the strength. Only a few weeks more and he is gone. At the ebb and swell of each new wave of remembrance, the young woman's own salt tears surge forth to fill a sea of sorrow.

*****

BINGO! On a hot summer night her Nanna is hoping to win big. Three months after her father's death, almost to the day, the young woman's remaining grandmother, collapses at Tuesday night bingo. The emergency response team react to what they believe is a coronary and her full fleshy white breasts with their fine lattice of tiny red veins are laid bare to the eager eyes previously fixed firmly on their dabbers and cards. The indignity of immodesty is unwarranted, she has not suffered a heart attack. She has reacted adversely to a powerful antibiotic, and she never regains consciousness.

*****

Under the white weight of an unexpected early winter storm, the man's only sister sits on the runway a long time waiting for the plane to park. It is pretty outside the small window, soft and silent, a bright white blanket over the usual grey and black of the busy airport tarmac. She turns her phone on. Her niece and the baby's father are at the hospital. If the driving conditions were better, they would be sent home. Looking out at the storm the aunt is comforted that the young couple are safely settled and will be staying at the hospital overnight. She is glad to have arrived, the six-hour flight behind her. She will be here for the baby's birth. She was too late in the spring to see her brother again. She is on time to welcome his first grandchild. She is the only one left to represent their side of the family tree.

Contractions began on Thursday evening, but twenty-four hours later there is precious little progress. There are complications: a C-section is required, and an infection is diagnosed. The frightened young woman is quick to tell the doctors about her grandmother's genetic abnormality. Both mother and baby test positive for long QT syndrome, the congenital condition that resulted in her grandmother's death. The surgeon reassures her that she has no cause for concern. With tears of gratitude, the exhausted mother-to-be whispers, "Thank you."

Sheltered by the hall-width double doors to the surgery ward the proud new father carefully cuddles his new baby girl. Just minutes after her birth she mimics him as he demonstrates how to stick out her tongue at the crowd of onlookers peering through the large glass barrier. Her guardian angels smile at her defiant gesture of greeting. Hooray for Hazel, this petite and perky newborn, namesake of her paternal great-grandmother, is the rich remainder of the woman whose haloed hazel irises often sparkled with mischievous independence.

Hazel is a tenacious tribute to those who are not present to inhale the sweet scent of her silky soft skin or share her parent's joy as they cradle the cherished child, safe and alive.

Author's Afterward:

This story is a work of autobiographical fiction, a combination of autobiography and fiction. While the characters and sequence of events are borrowed from my own life the details and intimate internal images are imagined. This story was written to support my own healing process after the death of my younger brother.

Susan Diane

<u>Legacy of Love</u>

I sit cross-legged to meditate
Your warm weight settles against my thigh
My arm rests on your back
Your paw in my palm
You are not alone
I am bereft, bereaved and you are not yet left.
How heavy my heart is, while you are leaving me.
How heavier it will be when you are gone.
Without words silently you love, unconditionally.
Sad, I remember each moment when I have betrayed this love.
A cross word, an angry refusal, it is easy when you return, un recriminating.

There is no reprieve for the agony of losing you.
You will remain etched forever in my heart,
My soul aches in anticipation of your absence.
All you ever wanted from me was more time and attention.
Now all I want is more time with you, to give you my attention.

Reluctantly, gratefully, I accept what is.
You have earned your rest.

Norm, thank you for your support! Hope this helps mend some broken pieces! em :)

EMILIE WHITE

I am Emilie White, a daughter, a sister, a wine enthusiast and event/wedding coordinator.

I love and appreciate every moment spent with family and friends while creating new memories with them. I am honoured to be writing my second chapter, with the ability to open up about a sensitive topic and to also be sharing this experience with so many family members.

Special thanks to my mom for always being the best inspiration and guiding light in helping me put my broken pieces together.

Forever Changed

MY GRIEF BRAIN DUMP
BY EMILIE WHITE

In College one of my professors guided us through weekly "brain dumps" where we would just talk and share about anything that was on our mind and needed to get off of our chest. It didn't have to make sense as long as we left feeling lighter. So, this is my grief brain dump. Everything that comes to mind and what I feel when I think of grief.

Meredith Grey once said "Grief comes in on its own time for everyone, its own way. So, the best we can do, the best anyone can do, is try for honesty. The really crappy thing, the very worst part of grief is that you can't control it. The best we can do is try to let ourselves feel it when it comes."

Grief is how we respond to loss. It isn't just death we grieve. It's life. It's loss. It's changes. The loss of relationships and friendships. Everyone responds differently and how they react to and overcome their grief is different. Grief is something everyone feels, but how we grieve is what sets us apart.

Personally, I respond to most grief by feeling broken. Like a sheet of glass completely shattered. It's not something that can be easily fixed and just put back together at the flip of a switch. It takes time, piece by piece, to overcome the emotions and realities. Every piece of that shattered glass is a memory, a story, a feeling that needs and deserves to be felt and remembered. It's okay to feel broken as long as you know how to recreate yourself after.

Emilie White

Recreate a version of yourself that can live and move on after that loss. I know from my experiences that it's so much harder said than done.

The reason I think being broken is okay is because we can only grow and get stronger from there. I once heard at a conference the speaker say that we have to be broken to grow. Think of a seed, it starts in a dark, deep place and breaks and cracks in order to grow and see the light.

Everyone needs a moment of being a seed to blossom into the person they are meant to be.

We need to grieve the person, the situation, and the moment in order to heal and put our broken pieces together again.

I have felt loss. I have been so broken. I can honestly say I have been broken because I know how absolutely amazing it is to be whole.

I want to normalize the feeling of grief and loss after the end of a romantic relationship. I have experienced grief in a way I had never thought possible. After spending so many years with someone, opening up, sharing dreams and dreaming about what your life will look like, for all of it to just be gone is unimaginable. When you're dating someone, you aren't in that relationship in hopes of it being over one day. You are with that person to build a life with and hope that they are yours forever. I grieved the life I thought I'd have. The trips I thought I'd take. The family I dreamed I'd have. I grieved the memories we made, and I grieved him. I still do. I fall fast and love hard, making it even harder to fall out of love with someone. This is me healing and overcoming my emotions and putting some of those broken pieces together. After over a year, I am still recovering and learning to let go. I thought I found my forever, instead, I've found myself again.

Friendship breakups are a bitch and grieving them has been a part of growing up for me. It's so difficult to navigate friendships in your 20s. They are some of the most transitional years. I've come to accept the fact that some friends will come and go and that's okay and normal. Friends come at different stages in life and some simply stay in that chapter of life. I have spent a long time and put the effort into friendships that simply didn't deserve it. It's something I wish I had learned a lot sooner in life.

Grandpa, Grandma and Pépère not a day goes by that I don't think about each and every one of you. I miss and love you all. Keep looking down and shining your light on me.

To the grandparents who weren't mine by blood, I miss you both and am forever thankful for the stories you shared with me.

Simply writing this chapter is part of my grieving. I am able to talk about it and let people know how I was feeling through everything. Slowly but surely picking up those broken pieces of glass, finding who I am and who I wish to be. Focusing on the step in front of me instead of the whole staircase, grieving with the support of friends and family. Although I am someone who generally deals with emotion internally, I have learned how important it is to have a support system, someone to help pick up those pieces of broken glass. Meredith Grey, a fictional character in the series Grey's Anatomy influenced me to write this chapter. She goes through more loss than anyone else in the whole Grey's Anatomy series. She grieved family members, friends, patients, children, jobs and even herself. It just goes to prove that we can overcome anything, and grief is simply a part of life and that we don't have to go through anything alone.

"There's an end to every storm. Once all the trees have been uprooted. Once all the houses have been ripped apart. The wind will hush, the clouds will part, the rain will stop, and the sky will clear in an instant. But only then, in those quiet moments after the storm, do we learn who was strong enough to survive it." – Meredith Grey

A SEED BREAKS OPEN AND
DISSOLVES INTO THE GROUND.
ONLY THEN DOES A
NEW FIG TREE COME INTO BEING.
THAT IS THE MEANING OF
DIE BEFORE YOU DIE.
~ RUMI

BRITTANY STARR

My name is Brittany, I am 32 years old Mother of 2 healthy strong boys and 2 that have passed on. I've dedicated my life thus far to helping others and personal development. I come from a very complicated family dynamic of being raised in and out of the foster care system and having my "adopted" family, who showed me the true meaning of love. I am a survivor of domestic violence and have had my fair share of up and down moments in life, that I am not too proud of, but those moments made me who I am today

HEALING THROUGH GRIEF
BY BRITTANY STARR

As I write this, it makes me reflect on my own personal grief, and I'm proudly looking at where I am now compared to where I started 10 years ago. There is hope, and you will get there just like I did. When people think of grief most people tend to relate it to death, when it is so much more than just death.

Grief can be the end of a friendship, loss of employment, loss of financial security, ending of a romantic relationship... Grief can be the loss of something that has meant a lot to you in more ways than one (in my opinion). As we go through grief there comes a time when we need to face reality and see what it is doing to us as a person. (Harsh but true)

As we go through grief we may experience anger, denial, confusion, depression, etc. As we experience these feelings they affect us, we lose our "hop in our step", our "sparkle in our eye", so to speak.

When going through the grieving process, most people struggle with the stage of depression. It is a normal feeling and we all cope differently. (By all means, if you need to seek medical attention, please do so.) Just remember this is not the end. There are ways to get through it.

Experiencing grief isn't easy, but it is important to acknowledge what needs to be done to make it through the grief and come out of it with your sanity and peace.

As mentioned, there are many stages of grief and, in my opinion, healing from grief should start with acknowledging your pain first and foremost. We need to feel those emotions. Scream, cry, punch a pillow, seek therapy or reach out to your support system, put it on paper and burn it.. just acknowledge it.

Focusing on your healing sometimes feels selfish but it's not! IT IS A MUST!

We cannot be the best versions of ourselves if we don't heal. Even though we're still going on every day as a parent, an employee/employer, a spouse, a caregiver, we are not fully attentive while we're struggling with our grief.

Some techniques you can try to use for healing:
Self-care; pamper yourself, do something you enjoy for yourself and no one else, go for a walk in nature and ground yourself. If you can't get outdoors, do a guided Grounding Visualization Meditation, or reach out to someone, you can talk to a therapist, get counselling, and find a support system. Journaling is an excellent way of letting go. Speaking your grief out loud or putting it on paper is a great way of releasing it. Going to the gym or doing yoga, or even hiring a life/wellness/grief coach can be beneficial. You could even colour, or paint. Even just dance.

Many times people won't truly understand your grief, as our grief is unique to each of us and that's okay. The fact that they want to be there and listen to show you that love and compassion is all we need sometimes. If someone has experienced similar grief, lean on them and ask them what worked for them.

Finding a professional that you vibe with is also important. You may not find the right therapist immediately but don't give up.

Healing from grief isn't going to happen overnight; it may take months or even years. You may be triggered throughout your healing journey and that's okay! It will be painful mentally, emotionally and spiritually. All of us grieve differently. We all heal differently. What works for me may not work for you, but don't give up, you will find something that works for you. I hope there is something you can take from this, whether for yourself or for someone else.

In the beginning, you will more than likely need to dedicate a lot of time to your healing and ensuring you are staying present with these current emotions, over time it will require less and less work. You will develop techniques that work for your triggers, and your feelings of hopelessness, low energy, anger, and resentment, among many other negative emotions will diminish. You just need to be patient with yourself. Speak kindly to yourself. Treat yourself in a kind and gentle manner. It's okay to not be okay. Listen to your body. take the rest you need and work on your healing.

Brittany Starr

Note: if you ever have thoughts of harming yourself or harming others please seek professional help because you matter, sometimes we don't think it but it is a true statement. You do matter!

You matter to me.

Emotional Symptoms of Grief

Denial
Sadness
Anger
Guilt
Helplessness
Numbness
Yearning
Relief
Loneliness
Anxiety
Obsession

Physical Symptoms of Grief

Overwhelming tiredness and exhaustion
Confusion
Difficulty with Concentration
Sleep changes
Appetite changes
Nightmares
Crying
Social Isolation
Restlessness
Aches and Pains
Anxiety attacks
Difficulty Breathing

Forever Changed

STEPHANIE DAWSON

Stephanie Dawson is a grief coach, death doula, writer, mother, and grandmother. She blogs at substack and is on most social media as Stepping Stones EOL Doula Services.

Stephanie enjoys her family, travel, reading, and time with friends. She lives in Minnesota.

LOVE, GUILT, AND GRIEF
BY STEPHANIE DAWSON

Everyone knows grief makes you sad, right? Angry sometimes. I didn't expect the amount of guilt. Although, thinking about it, I probably should have. I've suffered from grief guilt since I was 4 years old when my sister Lisa died. Guilt for not being a better sister, as smart as my sister, even survivor's guilt for daring to be alive. Since then, I've experienced a lot more loss; divorce, my home, a career that I loved and worked hard for, my health, then the death of my only son, quickly followed by the death of my mother, in less than a 2-year period. There has been so much guilt to work through, partly because of anger (how dare they leave?).

We were divorced when my children were 14 and 11, in 2002. I say "we" because we all got divorced, kids included. My ex-husband was abusive and cruel. One night, he slammed my tired son's elbow into the dinner table because it was on the table while he was eating. Then my son immediately covered his head with his hands -- and my heart froze, what happened in this house when I was away? I was away a lot at the time, in nursing school with 3 jobs to put myself through, I had to believe everything at home was fine.

We left that same night, no regrets.

Raising kids on your own isn't easy, I had to work a lot, plus I was dealing with a lot emotionally, leading to drinking too much when I was home. A year later, at a football physical, my 12-year-old son's blood pressure was 190/140, lying down. We went from a simple physical to paediatric intensive care an hour away. It was scary. After that, unrelated, my 15-year-old daughter started throwing up every time she ate, and to this day she still throws up a lot; nobody knows why.

Over the next several years, a lot of things happened. My daughter had an accident and lost a large portion of her vision - she can see some, just not well enough to drive or read a book. I was injured at work, then had swine flu and developed fibromyalgia and spondylitis, so I'm now disabled. My son met a lovely girl whom he married and had 4 beautiful and smart children with.

He still suffered from heart problems and hypertension and was discovered to be bipolar. He was also an alcoholic, which is a quite common method of self-medicating with Bipolar Disorder.

He died on January 5th, 2020. I miss him every day. Until then, I had lived close and babysat at least once a week, having sleepovers with the grands once or twice a month, and frequent family nights with dinner and a movie, board games, walks and fun outings. At her request, my daughter and I moved in with my daughter-in-law and grandchildren to help out, but that wasn't a long-term solution and almost 2 years later, we moved an hour away from them. We see them as often as we can.

Stephanie Dawson

There was a lot of guilt for working so much, arguing with him due to my expectations, and for not keeping him alive through sheer force of will. I mentally chastised myself for every time I said "no" or "not right now" his whole life. I felt guilty the first time, and every time I felt joy, until I realized how much he loved all of us, and how proud he'd be to see us thriving, not just surviving.

My mom suddenly got sick and died, a little over a year later. Looking back, it was obvious she hadn't been well for quite some time, but she had just turned 74 and none of us were worried. She had always been fiercely independent, living on her own and keeping an eye on herself. She had type 2 diabetes and a heart condition - she had to have stents put in, and managed to live almost a decade after.

We hadn't really talked for quite some time. She liked conspiracy theories and I'd debunk them, which made her really mad. People often say to not speak ill of the dead, but truth is always truth, we weren't close. When I was 15, I overheard her telling my aunt that she had never wanted kids and didn't like them. Suddenly, my whole life made more sense as not everyone is cut out for motherhood. It was still another 20 years or so before I stopped seeking her approval, which caused a wider rift. Even though she didn't care for motherhood, she doted on her 6 grandchildren. She loved spending time with them, and they love her. Having a difficult relationship like that leads to so much death guilt, and really complicated grief.

You don't recover from grief, you learn to live with it and around it. You can work through it. It takes a lot of love to

Stephanie Dawson

heal, and through love, and forgiveness, for them and for yourself you will find your way. Don't put too much stock into the day-to-day, just keep going. One day, you'll look up, and see how far you've come.

After all, you're still here, and you have so many wonderful things yet to do.

Stephanie Dawson

Forever Changed 111

MELANIE JOANNETTE

My name is Melanie Joannette. This is my second time participating in this beautiful adventure. I am as equally excited this time as the first. I find great joy in spending time with my husband, family, friends and my dogs. Rain or shine and even -20's, outdoors is where I ground myself, feel liberated and closest to my higher power. Playing music is where I naturally express myself, whether it is with loved ones or by myself. Of course, I always have my favourite spectators with me, my dogs!

GIFTS
BY MELANIE JOANNETTE

Grief! Such a small 5 lettered word with immense emotions attached to it. Nobody is insusceptible to it.

Whether it's the loss of loved ones, life obstacles, a relationship that has ended, health issues, or the passing of beloved pets, grief is a universal stage of life and doesn't discriminate. When it comes to losing loved ones, I have lost some special souls, from family to friends, grandparents and my father-in-law, who all played great roles in my life. All of them taught me different things in life and at different stages. I think the acknowledgement of this is a healing part of grief. To acknowledge and be grateful that even if something we knew has ended in one shape or form, we are still whole and richer for it, as we hold on to the gifts that were offered to us by these precious souls. When I say gifts, I mean love, support, security, hope, life lessons and life tools.

The same goes with life obstacles. They are a part of the grieving cycle. They say there are 5 stages to grief. Denial, anger, bargaining, depression and acceptance. We all can relate to that no matter what life has presented to us. For me, health issues have definitely made me live through these stages.

Denial= This is not happening to me.
Anger= I hate that this is happening to me.

Melanie Joannette

Bargaining= If I take better care of myself, please let this go away.
Depression= I can't do this.
Acceptance= I need to work with what I got so I can move forward.

With this journey, I can also relate to grieving the loss of my career and certain activities that I enjoyed and identified myself with. It's funny how as I am writing and revisiting all of this, it no longer has any importance to me or importance to my identity, seeing where I am at now through the healing journey. At the same time, these sorrows are actually what made me who I am today, and I find that it's not about identity but more about discovering your new self. I have also found gifts in these grieving stages. These particular gifts are the support I had and still have from loved ones, the strength and willpower I unleashed, discovering new activities and having more time to help family and friends. Finding new purpose is my biggest gift in this process.

Grieving pets! Oh boy! I have had my fair share of that! Always telling myself this is the last time I am going through this. Somehow, always ending up getting another four-legged fur ball of love. I read a long time ago, "To love and be hurt often, and to love again- this is the brave and happy life!" And do they ever bring happiness into our lives! The gifts in this are the teaching of compassion, unconditional love, forgiveness, living in the moment and most importantly, experiencing the moment.

Melanie Joannette

At every death or ending, there is also a new beginning. When you see that, you then realize the healing that grief brings along with the rest of the emotions. Just like grief is attached to healing, healing is also attached to growth. The most precious gift of all.

With all of this, I find myself more equipped to serve and help others in need of support when it is their time of grieving.

Grief cannot be measured or have a time limit before you can start healing. Only when the person going through this is ready to go through the stages, can they decide when they are ready to see the gifts. No matter how hard it is to see someone you love going through this, you need to have faith that the process will eventually bring them to a new beginning and an abundance of joy and love.

We all have life purposes. Some are different then others. Some change as we grow. Some are short-lived when we lose beautiful souls. But, I believe we all have a common life purpose. That is to live in joy, love and to be loved, That is what the Greater Power wants for us all. Whether you call it the universe, God, Angels, Buddha....

May we all heal, be joyful, love and be loved.
Melanie

ANITA DJURKOVIC

Anita knows what it's like to experience both deep valleys and mountaintop views, but it is the deep valleys that have given her the ability to serve with a level of humility that makes others feel seen, heard, and loved right where they are. Marko, Anita's father-in-law always told her that she should become a priest, and she feels, to this day, that he is certainly guiding her path. Working in tandem with God's grace, Anita owns and operates Ethereal Energy Interfaith Officiants, where she gets to bring her deep roots of spiritual formation, her extensive education, and her compassion through understanding significant loss into people's most cherished ceremonies. Anita has not just overcome many challenges but she has used each one as a brick to build a sturdy foundation from which to serve. It is from here she can show others what is possible for them in their own lives.

TOOK THE LONG WAY HOME
BY ANITA DJURKOVIC

The five stages of grief are often explained in an extremely specific chronological way. They are often referred to as denial, anger, bargaining, depression, and acceptance. I have never understood that methodology myself, and I have experienced an incredible amount of grief throughout my life. Sometimes thinking that I was born, in grief and that I was called to live my entire life in it.

However, I do not discount the popular grief model, and I know that it has great foundations.

Many grieving people experience all the stages in perfect order and see the healing revealed through the acknowledgment of these steps. Others may revisit certain stages in this grief spectrum many times over, and that is ok. Grief is so individual and within the individual nature of grief, that is where disenfranchised grief becomes a painful reality.

This is when you do not feel like you are allowed to express yourself or your pain. Grief that is allowed only from the sidelines. A person's grief that is not acknowledged.

My father-in-law was one of those incredibly diverse and dynamic people that was passionate and lively, brutally unapologetic, and lived his life the way he wanted to. I have known him since I was 21 years old, long before he became my father-in-law. After years of a tumultuous relationship, I had the true honor of being the one who closed his eyes after he left this earthly plane to be with his maker.

In the moments after his death, I talked with him and congratulated him, for an exceedingly difficult job well done. Saying "I am so proud of you, excellent job dad! Now you get to go to heaven." I talked to him a bit longer as I fixed his blankets and held his hand letting him know that he would see his wonderful dog Max again, and his friends and brothers and Mother and all of those who had gone before. Honestly, I was strangely giddy, joyful, and jubilant. Feeling the Holy Spirit in that room and a brightness I had never experienced before. I was truly leaping for joy for him.

When I went out into the hall to look for the nurses on his floor, I startled them because even though I had been sitting with him for days, I was not full of despair and panic. I joyfully called them into his room so that they could share in this blessed moment.

But the thing about divine experiences is they do not always translate very well to someone who might have missed the moment or to someone who held a different type of relationship with that person. So, I suppose the grief skipped me and began when I had to drive the short way home from the nursing home, early that morning, to be with my husband, to tell him about the news before he arrived at the nursing home that morning, as he had been for days before.

Of course, my husband was aware of this moment approaching, for we all were waiting for his passing, taking shifts over the last days, with other family members to be by his bedside. However, walking up on those patio steps to see my husband sitting waiting is when the complex reality of disenfranchised grief began.

I do not know if in those aforementioned stages of grief, or within any other model, anyone speaks of how two people can go in two completely different directions over the same loss. My husband comes from an extraordinarily rich Orthodox background, steeped in ancient traditions, and when it comes to grieving and death, the rites and rituals certainly aid in the healing of the family. I do not. My experience of being of English heritage was much stiffer. I may have witnessed the shedding of a tear, but there was not much outward and authentic outpouring of grief or expression.

When my husband became drawn closer to his culture and those who loved him and his father, I started to feel entirely left out. Like my unique relationship did not matter, my grief did not matter.

There are many important observances post-funeral in the Orthodox tradition. There is a first period of 40 days and then the mourning period lasts for an entire year, but my husband had to mourn with the people with whom he shared language and culture. And where he felt comforted by his people. I felt painfully alone.

So, I decided to live into my grief experience once again. But this time in a very constructive way.

Anita Djurkovic

I decided to plant and nurture a seed of hope that my father-in-law, Marko, had given to me many years before he died. He always said that I should become a priest. So, with my grieving, I chose to pick up that seed and see if it would grow. I dove headfirst into learning everything I could about serving as a woman Religious, and I became incredibly absorbed within the culture of my ancestral spirituality, instead of resenting my husband's experience.

I realized this had been something deeply missing from my life. I, in my learning, witnessed the beauty of spirituality in the acts of ceremony, and began to understand the importance of honouring a person when they die.

For a long time, even though I was a believer from an incredibly early age, because of my own wounds, I would say I did not ever want a funeral when I died. I never wanted anyone to come to see me. I did not even want to have a newspaper article about me, it was unnecessary. But between witnessing how my husband's family and friends came together to honour Marko, and with my eyes now opened to my calling, things rapidly began to change.

Now there was a realization within this grief that we all deserved to be honoured, celebrated, and remembered. Our memory is where we hold our love for someone forever. However, not everyone is lucky enough to have a large cultural understanding and a supportive community. Or a tradition where they may feel accepted, so that is where I now have the privilege to take what I have learned from this experience, and translate it into a second stage of life's calling. To make sure that anyone, no matter their

Anita Djurkovic

circumstances, can be honored and given the beautiful tribute and blessed burial that they deserve, when they too get to get to the other side where it is always beautiful, and bright and where we will grieve no more.

WILLOW ROSE

Willow Rose is a peripheral visionary who believes in the power of well-chosen words, the importance of mindful living, and that healing and redemption are possible for all beings. Willow, a once high school dropout and single mother, used the power of hope to return to school for her diploma; subsequently graduating summa cum laude with a Bachelor's Degree in English. She dedicated her teaching career to adults who had given up on education, and she used her own story to motivate and inspire her students. Willow, now retired and living near Tampa, Florida, shares a sense of wonder with friends through poetry and mindfulness while teaching that redemption is possible for us all in the infinite classroom of the You-niverse. Namaste

MAITRI: SELF-COMPASSION DURING TIMES OF GRIEF
BY WILLOW ROSE

"The deeper sorrow carves its furrows upon your soul, the more joy it can contain."
-Kahlil Gibran

For Saffra

The body of a sea anemone is soft and open, its luminous tentacles waving peacefully in the current, a jewel of the sea. Yet if we were to put our finger near it, it would close up and become hard and impenetrable. Everything does that spontaneously, and we, as human beings, reflect the same instincts to protect ourselves when confronted with unpleasant, uncomfortable feelings, particularly when we feel grief. Yet when we remain soft and open to grief, we can experience growth and develop "maitri," the Sanskrit word for unconditional friendship with oneself leading to self-compassion extending out to others. Thus, when we allow ourselves to feel grief, no matter how painful, we feel the totality of what it is to be human and to be fully alive.

Part of being human is that we regard discomfort in any way as negative - feelings like disappointment, embarrassment, irritation, resentment, anger, jealousy, fear, and most potently painful of all the emotions, grief. Pema Chodrun, the beloved Buddhist monk, has written extensively about this very subject, and in her book, *When Things Fall Apart*, she writes, "Someone needs to encourage us not to brush aside what we feel, not to be ashamed of the love and grief it arouses in us. Not to be afraid of pain. Someone needs to encourage us: that this soft in us could be awakened and that to do this would change our lives."

"It's also very helpful to realize that this very body that we have sitting right here right now... with its aches and its pleasures... is exactly what we need to be fully human, fully awake, fully alive," Pema writes, and she goes on to give us a template on how we can begin to open ourselves to maitri.

Mindfulness meditation and repetitions of positive affirmations are the ways to begin the practice of maitri. Loving-kindness meditation, also known as metta meditation, combines these two practices in a way specifically designed to cultivate maitri and it can help at any time during the grieving process.

It was twelve years ago when my beloved little sister, Jeannine, died suddenly. I had just spoken to her the night before and made plans to get together later in the week. She was my confidant, best friend and partner in crime. We were seventeen months apart and joined at the soul, not just at the hip. I loved her fiercely. Yet, I was so anesthetized by drugs and alcohol at her wake and funeral that it all seemed to be happening to someone else other than me, and now I barely remember it at all. I was so confused that when I arrived at her viewing I thought my other sister was her and that they had all played a terrible joke on me! Everything was completely surreal. And for weeks afterward I numbed myself with anything and everything I could find. When my little brother, Jeffrey, died just three years later I had cleaned myself up and felt the full impact of grief not only for him but for my Jeannine as well. I had kept my feelings at bay for so long, never getting around to grieving for her and it was like losing her for the first time. My brother's death opened the door to all I had suppressed. It also made me confront the feelings of shame over my actions at my sister's funeral; those feelings I had kept in a closed basket like a poisonous rattlesnake. They had been trapped there for years, coiled and ready to strike. When the bite came, it nearly killed me with regret, the pain was unbearable. And yet it forced me to begin seeking a spiritual path as the loss of a loved one often does, and by beginning my practice of maitri, I have come to grips with my loss and defanged the poisonous rattlesnake I called shame and grief. This is the other side of grief, the side that takes pain as the shell encasing our understanding and cracks it open so we feel it in all its terrible beauty and truly know what it is to suffer, to feel pain and pleasure and welcome them both equally so that we are completely open to all of life, and to feel what it is to be fully alive. Pema Chodrun calls it "opening the gates of compassion" and by allowing ourselves to feel grief for ourselves we begin to feel it for everyone who is feeling the same, knowing we are not alone.

In the book *The Prophet* by Kahlil Gibran he expresses the concept of maitri beautifully, writing, "Your pain is the breaking of the shell that encloses your understanding. Even as the stone of the fruit must break, so that its heart may stand in the sun, so must you know pain." And there is certainly nothing more painful than grief. I was determined not to feel the pain of my sister's death, not to feel the pain of anything and to allow only pleasure into my life but I relegated myself to what Gibran calls, "the seasonless world where you shall laugh, but not all of your laughter, and weep, but not all of your tears."

In other words, I was only half alive. Pain and pleasure are opposite sides of the same coin, and it is the currency we use to pay for a life that is lived not as if we were asleep in the snow, but awake to the intensity of all our emotions, awake to the good and the bad and all it means to be completely, unequivocally human.

When my best friend lost her sister a year ago, I began to understand, vicariously, the grieving process I had denied myself when I lost my sister all those years ago. As I watched her suffer, the "gates of compassion" opened and I began to be aware not only of her pain but my own as well. The empathy we share for one another has forged an unbreakable bond between us, a bond fired in the furnace of pain that has opened up both of us to the joy of a deep, unconditional friendship, a sisterhood that completes and fulfills us and reveals the paucity of the many other friendships that came before. Through her, I have come to accept how grief becomes a lifelong companion, never leaving in the beginning, softened over time, but never leaving completely. I have seen how the loss can visit us, sometimes when we least expect it, and the pain and the memories come cascading down, an unstoppable tsunami of emotion. It is self-compassion that keeps us from being swept away in the treacherous waters, and compassion for others that gives us not only a lifeline, but a lifeline, and we kick to the surface appreciating the gulps of sweet air in ways we never have before.

When we stay with our grief, and our broken hearts, we begin to realize life is always in transition.

There is both joy and sorrow in it and Kahlil Gibran invites us to remember they are inseparable, that "together they come, and when one sits alone with you at your board, remember that the other is asleep upon your bed."

Sticking with that uncertainty, and getting the knack of relaxing in the midst of chaotic emotion is how the practice of maitri can lead us to a spiritual path full of healing and love. By remaining as soft and open as the sea anemone and refusing to close up and become hardened to grief, we become open to feeling what it is to be wonderfully, terribly alive. We no longer just go through the motions but open ourselves to joy and sorrow, and the deeper meaning of life that we begin to perceive when we awaken and become truly alive. Grief is a doorway we all must pass through, sooner or later, and if we just keep it open, compassion and kindness toward others can flower and carry its sweet fragrance throughout the world, making it a better place for not only ourselves, but others as well. In this way we are forever changed, healing the world and ourselves through our grief.

IANTHA JINKS

Hi, I am, Iantha Jinks, I'm married, with two amazing adult children, who with their wonderful spouses have blessed us with three beautiful & brilliant granddaughters. This year marks 16 years since my husband and I said "I do!" and officially started our lifelong dance together. We have danced on many beaches in the Caribbean, at the Mayan Ruins, on Parliament Hill in Ottawa, in 10 countries, 3 Provinces, 7 States and even in Dollarama or grocery stores if a special song comes on the radio. I have recently retired from my daily job and we own a business. I love dancing with my husband, playing with my granddaughters, beadwork, painting, carving and of course writing! So my advice to you is: 'Find your hot button and dance all over it!" We are now using our life experiences to help coach others and point them to God! You can contact me via Facebook or email: jinksleadership@gmail.com

IANTHA JINKS

<u>No Flowers for Shelby</u>
No Flowers were sent to welcome your arrival,
No Flowers were sent to acknowledge your departure.
No cards were mailed to announce you were born,
No cards were mailed your death to mourn.
No newspaper ad read of your birth,
No newspaper Obituary read of your passing.
No tears of joy they shed for you,
No tears of sadness stained their cheeks.
No hugs to congratulate me for my new addition,
No hugs can comfort me for my loss.
You came and went, they didn't notice,
Not a ripple in life's sea did you make.
But now in my heart a storm rages,
For I am the only one who knows you, my Dearest Shelby!

It has been over 30 years but when I read these poems it feels like just yesterday. I was 5 months pregnant with my second child, our son was four years old and had just started JK. We had just gone away for the weekend on a shopping trip for maternity clothes, as I was just starting to show. That Monday I had a routine ultrasound appointment, back then we didn't get pictures, to find out the sex, or even take our spouses as people do now. It was simply a medical procedure to make sure everything was developing properly. My sister was babysitting our son and I took the bus to the appointment, as we only had one car. The appointment was pretty much uneventful but I did notice the technician was very quiet and didn't talk to me much at all. Oh well, I thought she must have been having a bad day! I took the bus back to my sister's to pick up our son and my husband met us there to drive us home.

As we walked in the door the phone was ringing, this was in the time before cell phones, so I hurried to answer it. It was my family doctor, he called to say he had to see us right away, no it couldn't wait it had to be that night. So back to my sister's to drop off our son and then the long drive to the doctor's office. My mind, how it raced, why was he calling, what was happening, was I having twins, my sister had twins, or was something wrong with our baby? By the time we arrived at the doctor's office it was way past his normal office hours, so why was he staying late just to see us? This was all so strange.

We walked into the office and we were not taken into an examination room but into his private office. On the wall, I could see ultrasound pictures of what appeared to be a baby but not clear like they are now.

After we were seated the doctor explained that these pictures were our baby and that there was definitely something wrong with our baby. He explained that our baby was "Anencephalic," that this is a serious birth defect and that our baby had no skull. What did he mean our baby had no skull? I could see its little head. No, what I was seeing was just tissue, there was no bone.

"So what are you telling us, our baby will have to wear a helmet forever?" I actually asked this. Then he explained that our baby would never live outside of my body and that even coming down the birth canal could crush its little head. He would have no nerves to connect the brain to the rest of the body, so there would be no way for his brain to tell his heart to beat. But wait, I could feel his heart beating now, I could feel him moving inside of me, they had to be wrong. The doctor explained that it was only my body that was keeping his little body going at this time and there was NO way this little baby would ever survive outside of my body. NO this couldn't be true, I needed a second opinion. Of course, and the arrangements had already been made for me to see a specialist the next day! The drive home that night was a blur, I couldn't sleep. This couldn't be happening to me, not to my baby!

The appointment the next day went much the same as the previous night, An appointment was made for me to go into the hospital to have a "therapeutic abortion."

WHAT! No way I was having an abortion. I couldn't do that to my baby. The doctor said there was nothing else that could be done and, there was no reason to carry a baby for four more months that wasn't going to live and my husband agreed. I was in too much shock to object any further, after all, I wasn't a medical professional.

The next day, to take my mind off it, my Mom took me out for lunch and we went to the mall. It didn't take my mind off of anything and in fact every time I saw a pregnant woman I felt hatred burn up inside me.

"Why did she get to have a baby when my baby was going to die!" By the end of the afternoon, I had decided just to go along with the doctors and my husband because my baby wouldn't be happy inside me for four months of hatred. So the following Monday, just one week after this nightmare began, I entered the hospital. I was awake for the whole procedure, which was basically rapidly induced labour. From there I was taken to a ward with three other women who were having abortions that day. I listened and watched as these three other women were discharged, the procedure completed and away they went. But not me, I was still laying on this stretcher in pain, but nothing seemed to be progressing. Then all of a sudden there was a gush and there was blood everywhere but still, no baby was delivered. They got me out of bed to change the sheets and clean me up, so they sat me on the toilet. Of course, that is when my baby decided to come out and again there was blood everywhere. I was hysterical! They rushed me back to the operating room to get the bleeding stopped and to give me a blood transfusion. After losing my baby and almost dying myself, I was released from the hospital the next day, to go home and take care of my other son.

To everyone else, it was as if nothing had happened, or at least it felt like that to me. I was just to continue on like part of me had not just died. It was at that point that a friend contacted me. She had had a baby that was stillborn. She was starting a group for Moms who had lost babies, and she asked if I wanted to come. It was this woman who encouraged me to write down my feelings. I now encourage anyone who has experienced this kind of loss to reach out to a support group or grief share in your area. It will help more than you would ever think.

Iantha Jinks

Also, you never know what life has in store for you in the future. Little did I know at the time, only 7 months later, I would give birth prematurely to my little daughter who is now an adult with two babies of her own.

Here is some poetry I wrote during that time of deep grief. It is my hope and prayer that you too will find some healing through my words...

IT JUST ISN'T RIGHT!

How could it happen to one so small!
Who hadn't even been given a chance,
Not a breath did you breathe,
Not a touch did you feel,
Oh, but to me you were so real!!!
They all said was for the best,
So, they made me choose your destiny,
To have to choose to say 'Goodbye"
Without even being able to say "Hello"
Never to have you in my arms to cuddle!
My heart how it aches for you now,
But alas it's too late, the choice was made,
Never to have lived, or to die on your own,
Who was I to choose what was the best,
Why, oh, why did I go along with the rest?
To have lost you with never having you.
How can I express how this emptiness hurts,
God in His Wisdom, with His Perfect Plan
Up in Heaven perhaps as an angel you fly,
BUT IT JUST ISN'T RIGHT THAT MY BABY SHOULD DIE!

Iantha Jinks

Nothing Seemingly Changed

The earth still turns,
The sun still shines,
The wind still blows,
The clouds still float,
The seasons still change.
The car still runs,
The phone still rings,
The television still glows,
The clock still ticks,
The radio still sings.
The neighbours still come and go.
The church bells still ring,
The schools are still open.
The playgrounds are still full,
The children still laugh.
Life still goes on,
Nothing seemingly changed,
But my soul is now still,
My baby is gone forever,
Oh, why does everyone else's life go on unchanged!

Iantha Jinks

What is Alive?

Trees are alive,
Leaves are alive.
Flowers are alive,
Grass is alive,
Even weeds are alive!
Dogs are alive,
Cats are alive,
Birds are alive,
Fish are alive,
Even tadpoles are alive!
If it can grow it's alive,
If it can reproduce it's alive,
If it can breathe it's alive,
If it can move on its own it's alive,
If it has a metabolism it's alive!
Into this category, humans fit as alive,

Even our unborn have a metabolism,
They grow, breathe, move and someday reproduce.
My baby was, even though unborn,
Please allow me this time to mourn!

Iantha Jinks

Life Sentence

Please don't condemn me,
For I love you so.
Please don't condemn me
For taking your life,
Please don't condemn me
For I was ill-advised.
Please don't condemn me
For my sacrifice.
Please don't condemn me
For the mistake I made.
Please don't condemn me
For my ignorance
Please don't condemn me,
For my sentence now stands,
Life with the memories of my loss!

Iantha Jinks

Never Forgotten

My health has returned,
I'm regaining my strength,
The bruises have faded,
My face now has some colour.
My wedding rings I now can wear,
Old clothes now fit again,
All signs of maternity have now passed,
I've even gone on a diet.
I started back to work again,
It feels good to be useful,
Life is developing back into a routine,
But believe me you'll never be forgotten!

Iantha Jinks

BECAUSE!!!

Because you didn't feel him move,
He wasn't alive!
Because you didn't see his body,
He wasn't a baby!
Because you say it's for the best,
He is better off!
Because you didn't make the decision,
I shouldn't regret it!
Because you feel no pain,
I need no medication!
Because you feel the time is right,
I should be over it!
Because you feel no loss,
I should not mourn!

Empty Arms, Empty Cradle

My arms how they ache, they are so empty now
My breasts how they throb, with milk that will not be drunk.
My ears how thy strain, for a cry to
break through the stillness.
My heart how it hurts from the pain of this loss.
Just yesterday I could feel you move,
now my tummy feels empty and cold.
No baby to hold, no baby to feed, no baby crying.
In the corner sits your empty cradle!

THANK YOU

If you need help, please reach out. Grief can be overwhelming sometimes, but there is always a helping hand reaching out to guide you through.

You can contact your local health unit to find the best resources in your area.

Sincerely,

The Authors of Forever Changed: Healing through Grief, and the Women of AAAB.

Manufactured by Amazon.ca
Bolton, ON